AF316642

The British Raj

An Enthralling Guide to the Administration of India by Britain

Free limited time bonus

Stop for a moment. We have a free bonus set up for you. The problem is this: we forget 90% of everything that we read after 7 days. Crazy fact, right? Here's the solution: we've created a printable, 1-page pdf summary for this book that you're reading now. All you have to do to get your free pdf summary is to go to the following website:

https://livetolearn.lpages.co/enthrallinghistory/

Or, Scan the QR code!

Once you do, it will be intuitive. Enjoy, and thank you!

Table of Contents

Introduction

No other empire is talked about quite as much as the British Empire.

Stretching from one end of the globe to the other, with roughly a quarter of the world under its rule, it was said the sun could never set on the British Empire. Both impressive and mired in controversy, the empire's influence continues to be felt today, as Britain's colonial rule largely shaped the world as we know it.

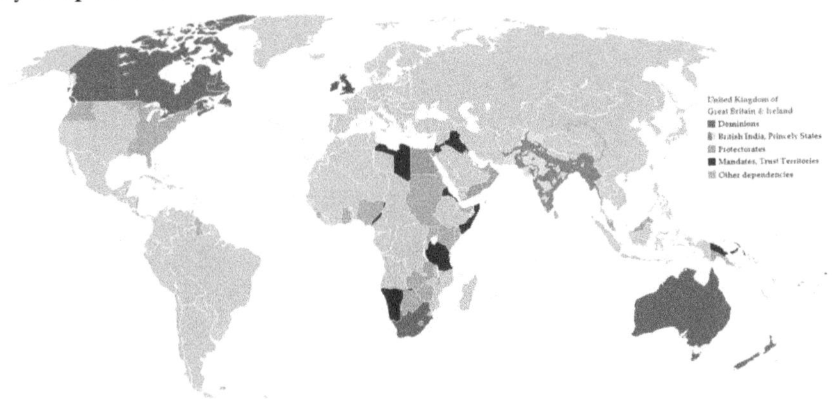

Map of the British Empire. [1]

One of the most important conquests for Britain was India, the jewel in the crown of its empire. Although Britain wouldn't officially "rule" India until the mid-1800s, the empire had its sights set firmly on the country as early as the 1600s, when the first group of British people arrived at Surat in 1608 with the British East India Company for trading purposes.

While Britain did not seriously consider colonizing at that time, the seeds had been sown. Over the next couple of hundred years, Britain slowly developed and strengthened its ties to the country and eventually formally took over.

The years between 1858 and 1947 are known as the British Raj, the period of time when India was directly under the British Empire's rule. During this time, India was influenced heavily by the British and went through a major transformation politically, socially, religiously, and culturally.

While many positives came out of Britain's influence, it was also a time marred by tension, violence, and instability. This book takes a closer look at the British Raj and considers questions like, what exactly is the British Raj? How did it come to be? What were the positives and negatives of Britain's rule in India? What did it mean for the native population? What was the chain of events that eventually led to the empire's end in India?

We'll examine the significant historical events and key players of this period and consider their contributions to the British Raj. We will conclude with a look at how Britain's colonization continues to impact present-day India.

Chapter 1: The Origins of Dominion

Britain's expansion and rise as the most powerful global empire by the 19th century is an astronomical feat given its size and location.

Motivated partially by financial interests and gain, Britain took slow, tentative steps toward expanding its empire in the 16th century. By the 18th century, rivalry with France had become an equally powerful driver of imperial ambition.

By the 17th century, explorers were given royal commissions to explore and establish settlements and colonies in the New World. With the exploration of the Americas, the British Empire began to expand in earnest as it traded across the globe and became deeply entrenched in the transatlantic slave trade.

Colonization of India

Britain's colonization of India did not happen overnight or in a sudden swoop. It happened in phases over two centuries. It began with trading in the Asian continent and gradually evolved into increased control by the East India Company over roughly a century (1757–1858).

Starting in 1858, Britain removed the British East India Company from the picture and began to rule India directly, a period known as the British Raj.

East India Company

One of the most important players in the colonization of India was the British East India Company (EIC). It allowed Britain to exert extensive political and economic control over much of the subcontinent, changing its political, social, and economic landscape forever.

To understand how the EIC was able to exercise political control over large parts of the Indian subcontinent, we need to go back to the beginning and consider how the Company was created and the role it played in global trade.

The East India Company was established in 1600 by a group of merchants after they received a royal charter from Queen Elizabeth I. The Company was set up to operate out of Asia with the goal of facilitating trade with countries located in that part of the world, like China, Indonesia, and East Asia.

East India Company Coat of Arms. [2]

In exchange for a percentage of the profits to the British Crown, the EIC was given a monopoly to trade in the East Indies. However, the competition for trade in that part of the world was fierce. Pitted against the Dutch East Indies Company and countries like France, Spain, and Portugal, the EIC took some time to find its footing.

Since the Company didn't have unlimited funds at its disposal and was unable to pay its employees a good salary, it allowed employees incentives like permission to trade privately for their own interests.

The East India Company had already been trading with India for several decades, and in 1611, it had even built a trading station at Masulipatam. But with a stronger focus on India, in 1639, the EIC acquired land from a local Nayak ruler and constructed Fort St. George, shifting its operation from Masulipatam to the newly built fort.

The location of the fort in Madras (modern-day Chennai) made it easier to purchase goods from the weaving centers, which were then exported to other countries. By the mid-18th century, Fort St. George was serving as the EIC's headquarters in southern India. The fort made trade easier and encouraged British settlers to settle in India. These developments facilitated the rapid expansion of trade.

Fort St. George in Madras.[8]

From the 16th century until the early 18th century, much of northern India was ruled by the Mughal Empire. When British traders arrived, Mughal rulers were initially welcoming, as they saw the financial benefits of trading with each other. Since the EIC held a royal charter, it had some political pull, which worked in its favor with the Mughals and Indian rulers, who were not shy about asking the EIC to interfere in regional wars or accept bribes.

The Mughals gave the East India Company trading rights, allowing British people to have access to affordable textiles, spices, and tea. In exchange, the British brought products from Europe to India. It felt like a win-win situation for both sides, as they reaped vast profits. The hugely successful East India Company enjoyed a rapid rise to power.

The EIC used its connections and resources to establish a vast trading network throughout the continent. Hot commodities like cotton, spices, tea, and opium were traded. It wasn't long until the East India Company had established itself as a dominant global player.

As its power grew, so did Britain's interest in India. As trading proved to be more than fruitful, Britain began to look at how the EIC could have influence over India in other ways. Before long, Britain's imperialist ambitions were being achieved.

East India Company Army

As time went on and the Company expanded, the number of trading posts grew, and the EIC faced increasing threats from rival nations like the French and the Indians, who were opposed to these British settlements.

Through 17th-century royal charters, the East India Company gained authority to maintain armed forces and wage war in Asia. Initially, these armies were small groups of soldiers assigned to trading posts to protect their assets and manage their security. Over time, the groups were expanded, and the EIC eventually created the East India Company Army. While the officers were British, the bulk of the soldiers were Indian. These Indian soldiers were referred to as sepoys. A steady stream of funds allowed the army to not only grow into one of the largest armies in Asia but also to create its own navy, the Bombay Marine.

The private army was used to maintain British power and control over the natives, defend against enemy attacks, and fight proxy battles. For example, during the Seven Years' War with France, Britain used the East India Company Army to fight against the French on Indian soil. In addition to protecting British interests in India, in the late EIC period, the army was sent to fight in wars in Burma, Egypt, and China.

The EIC's desire for greater control and power eventually caused friction with the Mughals and other rulers. By the 18th century, Mughal authority had significantly weakened, as it was faced with constant rebellions and internal conflict. The resulting instability created opportunities that the EIC exploited through warfare, alliances, and diplomacy. Rather than creating divisions outright, the EIC often exploited existing rivalries between regional powers, ensuring kingdoms remained too fractured to mount a unified resistance.

The army was thus sent out to conquer land through whatever means necessary and would go on to play a pivotal role in the EIC, which went from a simple trading partner to an imperial power.

Battle of Plassey

The Battle of Plassey, fought on June 23rd, 1757, is seen as a major turning point in India's history, marking the beginning of the EIC's territorial expansion in India.

It was fought between the East India Company Army and Siraj ud-Daulah, the Nawab of Bengal (the title is comparable to emperor). The EIC had already expanded into Bengal, and when they tried to further expand their reach, Nawab Siraj ud-Daulah remained firmly opposed.

Siraj ud-Daulah felt threatened by the EIC's growing power, and he was angry that they were looking to take even more from him. Things came to a head in 1756 when, without permission from Siraj ud-Daulah, the EIC went ahead and fortified its trading post in Calcutta as a defense against the French in preparation for the Seven Years' War. While the war was primarily fought in the Americas and Europe, regional conflicts were fought in pockets across the world, including India.

The pro-French nawab, angered by his authority being flouted and dismissed, retaliated by attacking the trading center in Calcutta. He had thirty thousand foot soldiers with him, an additional twenty thousand on horses, and several hundred elephants. His army was easily able to capture the post, which was defended by only two hundred British men.

The captured soldiers and civilians were imprisoned in a cell that came to be known as the "Black Hole." According to British accounts, they were given no food or water and left in cramped, suffocating conditions that were made worse by the heat, though historians debate the exact number who died overnight. Their treatment caused an outcry amongst the British and led Robert Clive, a general in the East India Company Army, to face Nawab Siraj ud-Daulah in battle.

Clive arrived in Calcutta with roughly three thousand men, a mix of British troops and sepoys. They were vastly outnumbered by Siraj ud-Daulah's troops, but a combination of luck, better military strategy, and several groups within the nawab's army switching sides at the last minute led to a decisive victory for Clive and the East India Company Army with minimal casualties. This victory strengthened the EIC's dominance and control in India and significantly weakened France's position as a colonial power.

After Siraj ud-Daulah's defeat, he was captured by the very troops who had betrayed him and was executed. Following his death, Mir Jafar was installed as the nawab of Bengal under EIC influence. He was, in effect, a figurehead, with real control residing in the EIC's hands. In exchange for his service, Clive was given access to the nawab's treasure chest and returned to England with an enormous fortune. Plenty more of the nawab's wealth was shipped to Britain.

Battle of Buxar

While the Battle of Plassey laid the foundation for the EIC's rule, the Battle of Buxar firmly cemented and established EIC dominance in eastern India. Fought on October 22nd, 1764, the battle was a culmination of simmering tensions in the area since the Battle of Plassey. Indian rulers were resentful of the EIC's growing power and authority and sought to put a stop to it.

These tensions escalated into a conflict between the East India Company Army and a group of Indian states—Bengal, Awadh, the Kashi Kingdom, and the Mughal Empire—that had formed an alliance. Even though the East India Company Army was vastly outnumbered, its troops, weapons, and strategies proved stronger, leading to a decisive victory over the Indian alliance.

This victory made the EIC the dominant military power in eastern India, but military success alone did not grant it legal authority to rule. A formal political settlement was required to secure its position.

In 1765, Robert Clive returned to India to resume his post as governor of Bengal. He was sent back to stabilize EIC rule after the upheaval of the war and to negotiate terms with the defeated powers. That same year, the Treaty of Allahabad was signed. Under the terms of the treaty, the Mughal emperor granted the EIC the Diwani rights (the right to collect revenue) in Bengal, Bihar, and Orissa in exchange for an annual payment. The nawab of Awadh was restored to his territory as a dependent ally, creating a buffer between EIC lands and the north.

This treaty marked the EIC's transition from a trading corporation with military influence to a territorial revenue-collecting power with formal political authority. Control of taxation meant control of the region's wealth. Over time, this system would open the doors for corruption, crime, and violence, have a severe negative impact on the native population, and eventually contribute to the EIC's downfall.

But for the moment, the EIC was at the height of its power. With military control, political recognition, and a steady stream of revenue, the EIC firmly established itself as the governing authority in Bengal and the surrounding provinces. When the British Parliament passed the India Act of 1784, increasing parliamentary oversight of EIC affairs while leaving administration in EIC hands, it became increasingly clear that India was falling under British imperial control.

East India Company's Rule (1785–1858)

Under the East India Company's rule, India went through a transformation, and every facet of society was impacted. Some of these changes were good, while others were detrimental. The key areas that were influenced were politics, the economy, and society.

Political Influence

India during the 18th century was largely divided into smaller empires and principalities with Indian princes as rulers. Over time, some princes were removed or became subordinate to EIC authority, while others were allowed to keep their positions with the understanding that their loyalty lay strictly with the EIC. More often than not, the princes complied, and in exchange, they enjoyed a life of wealth, comfort, and privilege.

This support of the princes and local rulers was necessary for the EIC as well, as it would have been nearly impossible for the Company to rule every part of India. This partnership allowed them to use a form of indirect governance and rule through people. On the surface, the local rulers governed their land and their people, but in reality, they had very little power and autonomy. The authority that was being enforced was that of the EIC.

This served a dual purpose. The EIC didn't have to handle the day-to-day issues, and the arrangement also served to appease those who believed they were being ruled not by a foreign authority but by their own people.

British legal institutions were introduced alongside existing religious and customary laws. There can be no doubt that implementing Western administrative practices made things easier and provided structure and order, but it also created confusion and unhappiness among the population, as they felt Western bureaucracy was designed to favor the "whites" or those who supported the British and the EIC.

Economic Influence

Historians will argue that the EIC's control helped to modernize India's economy. While there may be some truth to this, it is difficult to say for certain whether this was beneficial for the country in the long run.

Economically, while the EIC and its loyal supporters benefited greatly from its control and grew generational wealth, most of the country and its people were left devastated and struggling. Company revenue policies intensified economic pressure in many regions, and those who were already struggling financially were hit the hardest. The collection of taxes was one of many factors contributing to widespread poverty.

The East India Company had made no secret of the fact that it valued India's abundance of riches and raw natural resources. The EIC extracted substantial wealth and resources from the subcontinent during the decades it ruled over India. And the more it took, the more it wanted.

The Industrial Revolution started in Britain during the 1700s and completely transformed British society and the world at large. It would have a direct impact on India. Raw materials like cotton, coffee, and jute were taken from India to be used by factories in Britain to produce goods. The finished goods were then shipped back to India to be sold to Indians at a huge profit.

This amounted to untold riches and wealth, mostly for the EIC and those Indians directly involved with the East India Company. The demand for raw materials was so high that in some regions, the expansion of commercial crops reduced land available for subsistence farming.

Having found a profitable enterprise, the EIC was reluctant to share. It was determined to keep it all for itself, so it tightly controlled the export of goods and encouraged local people to purchase imported British goods, which further strained their meager finances. Local industries and tradespeople suffered as a result of the EIC's stringent trading policies and restrictions. Many people were forced to give up their way of living and find another source of income.

One aspect in which the EIC's economic policies had a positive impact was the country's infrastructure. While the roads, canals, and bridges were all built to facilitate the EIC's trade and transport and stimulate economic growth, they made things easier for the Indians too. Major railway expansion occurred later under Crown rule. These developments allowed for greater mobility, connected the vast country, and provided jobs.

Great Bengal Famine of 1770

A number of factors came together to contribute to widespread famines across the country. One that particularly stands out is the Great Bengal Famine.

This famine affected the provinces of Bengal and Bihar during the period of dual governance under EIC revenue control (1765–1772). Company revenue policies significantly exacerbated the crisis, as the famine occurred during a time when the EIC's collection of taxes placed enormous strain on the population.

Bad weather at that time led to a poor harvest, and whatever the farmers were able to harvest had to be sold to pay taxes to the EIC, leaving little to nothing in reserve for the farmers and the people. The EIC did nothing to help the farmers or provide any form of relief. Instead, revenue demands continued despite the crisis, and market speculation worsened food shortages. What's worse is that the EIC and the president of the Council at Fort William were warned about the dry season and the approaching famine by the naib nazim, the deputy of the nawab of Bengal.

The naib nazim worked closely with the EIC. They would be able to speak fluent English and be influenced by the British culture. They were responsible for collecting taxes from the people, governing the territories, and overseeing the general running of affairs. Worried about the impact of an encroaching famine, a proposal was made to the Council to collect grain in a different, more humane way.

The concerns, warnings, and the proposal were ignored. At one point, discussions were held to lower taxes to provide relief, but this, too, was scrapped. Instead, revenue demands were not substantially reduced despite widespread crop failures. What food was available was nearly impossible to buy due to the skyrocketing costs.

Everything snowballed together, and when the famine arrived in earnest, the scale of suffering was catastrophic. Estimates suggest that up to ten million people may have died, though figures remain debated. The famine contributed to the end of the dual governance, with the EIC taking over complete control.

The Bengal Famine is just one example of how the native population was treated. The resentment and anger toward the East India Company stemmed from these kinds of events, and as the decades went on, they would only worsen.

Social Influence

While some Indians saw the authority of the EIC as a way of amassing wealth by joining them or partnering with them, for the majority of the population, life under the EIC was one of hardship and brutality. Financial disparity also grew. Only a small percentage of the population, typically those closely associated with the British, were living lavish lifestyles. The greater majority struggled to provide the basic necessities like food, shelter, and education for their families.

Adding to their frustrations, they saw the erosion of their own customs, practices, and traditions. For the native population, rule under the EIC meant their way of life was being erased to be replaced by a Westernized system.

This clash between two radically different cultures created confusion, unhappiness, and further divisions within Indian society. To thrive and survive, one had to adapt, but to adapt meant giving up who one was.

Historians point out and argue that not all social reforms and changes were bad. For example, under the EIC, sati, a ritual practiced by Hindus where widows had to throw themselves on their dead husband's funeral pyre and burn to death alongside him, was abolished. In modern times, we can look at sati and easily see it as a barbaric and inhumane practice. Why should a woman have to be burned alive just because she was now a widow? However, for the Hindus, this was a deeply religious and spiritual practice. Some Indians certainly welcomed the reform, but others viewed it as yet another example of British interference in religious traditions.

The EIC also passed the Hindu Widows' Remarriage Act of 1856, which allowed widows to remarry. In many upper-caste Hindu communities, widows were discouraged or forbidden from remarrying. They were expected to live simple lives and were sometimes regarded as bad luck. Indian reformers campaigned vigorously for change, and the EIC ultimately supported legislation permitting remarriage. While the act did not immediately transform social attitudes, it was still an important shift and led to broader debates about social reform in India.

Child marriage was not abolished under EIC rule, though later reforms under the British Raj sought to restrict it. However, the EIC prioritized children receiving an education. Under the EIC, India's education system saw notable changes. In the final years of EIC rule, universities were established in 1857 in cities including Calcutta, Bombay, and Madras, mirroring Britain's education system. Professional careers like medicine and law were easier to attain, and with English promoted as the unifying language, many educated Indians were given jobs within the British administration.

Some policies promoted legal equality, but caste distinctions remained deeply embedded in society. However, these policies contributed to the emergence of an English-educated elite, creating a different kind of inequality in Indian society—the educated, Westernized class against the rest of the population. Those in rural areas were particularly unhappy with the changes and saw them as threats to their very existence, especially when Christian missionaries descended on India with the intent of converting Hindus and Muslims.

The Caste Disabilities Removal Act protected inheritance rights after conversion, meaning those who converted to Christianity would not lose their right to inherit land and property. Many people eagerly signed up, while others resisted, creating religious conflict and division.

Over time, the resentment and discontent toward the British became harder to ignore as Indians felt increasingly disrespected and discriminated against. They were treated like second-class citizens and, in extreme cases, as less than humans in their own land by people who were outsiders.

These feelings continued to simmer and grow until they finally came to a head on May 10th, 1857.

Rebellion of 1857

Although there had been earlier uprisings, 1857 marked the most widespread and serious challenge to East India Company rule. The Indians, who were deeply unhappy and had been for some time, lived with the abuse and injustice for decades until they couldn't take it anymore.

In addition to the political, economic, and social changes discussed previously and their long-term impact on the Indians, other factors came into play that led to the rebellion, such as the Doctrine of Lapse.

Under the Doctrine of Lapse, introduced by Lord Dalhousie, the Governor-General of India from 1848 to 1856, any princely state under East India Company authority would be annexed if its ruler died without a biological male heir. The EIC refused to recognize adopted heirs, despite long-standing Indian traditions. By enforcing this doctrine, the EIC took control of several princely states, including Satara, Sambalpur, Nagpur, and Jhansi. While the policy expanded EIC territory, Lord Dalhousie's aggressive policies were met with deep resentment and became one of the leading causes of the Indian Rebellion of 1857.

By the 1850s, it felt to the Indians like the British were simply everywhere, and the friction between the two sides continued to intensify.

Two Sepoys. Hand-colored engravings by Frederic Shoberl.'

The final straw came in the form of the Enfield rifle, which had been used by the British Empire for several years. In 1857, the EIC issued this rifle to the sepoys (Indian soldiers) in its army. Rumors soon began to circulate that the cartridges had been made with beef and pig fat. Because the cartridges had to be used by biting them open, Muslim and Hindu sepoys saw it as a grave disrespect and deeply insulting to their religious beliefs.

For Muslims, pigs were a forbidden animal, and for Hindus, the cow was sacred. To the sepoys, biting the cartridges and greasing them using their saliva felt the same as having to eat pigs and cows. Many sepoys were abused, overworked, underpaid, and subjected to brutality by the racist British, so this became the last straw and the catalyst for the rebellion.

In Meerut, when sepoys defied orders to use the new cartridges, they were promptly arrested and sent to prison. Outraged at this injustice, other sepoys followed suit, banding together and shooting their British officers.

The sepoys marched on Delhi, gathering support from other soldiers and civilians on the way. Once in Delhi, they were joined by the local garrison and quickly seized the city. In less than a day, they proclaimed Bahadur Shah II a symbolic emperor, and a full-blown rebellion began to spread like wildfire in northern India. Peasants, land owners, and soldiers took up arms, determined to stamp out British rule.

Capture of Delhi, 1857.[5]

Unfortunately for the movement, while it received significant support in parts of northern and central India, many Indian princes and local rulers refused to join and kept out of the conflict, leaving the sepoys and civilians to battle it out themselves.

Chapter 2: Consolidation of Power

Britain's Response to the Rebellion

After the initial element of shock and surprise wore off, the British moved quickly to regroup. Reinforcements were rushed in from Britain, while loyal troops from the Punjab and other regions were mobilized. What had begun as a mutiny among the sepoys soon grew into a much wider rebellion across northern and central India.

Some of the fiercest fighting occurred in major cities such as Delhi, Kanpur, and Lucknow. Delhi quickly became the symbolic center of the uprising after the rebels proclaimed the aging Mughal emperor, Bahadur Shah II, as their leader. British forces laid siege to the city for months before storming and recapturing it in September 1857. The fall of Delhi dealt a major blow to the rebellion, but the conflict was far from over.

In Kanpur, rebel forces led by Nana Sahib besieged British troops before one of the most infamous massacres of the rebellion took place, in which British prisoners, including women and children, were killed. News of the killings shocked Britain and enraged British troops in India, contributing to the harsh reprisals that followed.

Lucknow also became a major battleground. British forces held out in a fortified compound during a prolonged siege before relief forces arrived. Fighting in the region continued well into 1858. Meanwhile, in central India, resistance was led by figures such as Rani Lakshmibai and the rebel commander Tantia Tope, whose forces continued to challenge British control even after other rebel strongholds had fallen.

The rebellion lasted approximately fourteen months. The battles and regional conflicts were bloody, vicious, and often fought without mercy. The vastly superior British military resources gradually turned the tide. The killing of British women and children particularly enraged British troops, and they responded with severe reprisals. Public executions, including the notorious practice of blowing rebels from cannons, were carried out as a warning to others.

Around six thousand British soldiers and civilians were killed during the uprising, but the number of Indian casualties was far higher. Most scholarly estimates suggest between 100,000 and 200,000 Indians died in the fighting and reprisals that followed.

Slowly but steadily, British forces regained control of the regions that had risen against them. By mid-1858, it had become clear that the rebellion was collapsing. Disorganization among the rebels, the absence of unified leadership, and the military advantages enjoyed by British forces all contributed to their defeat.

The rebellion was militarily suppressed by mid-1858. On November 1st, 1858, Queen Victoria issued a proclamation formally transferring the governance of India from the East India Company to the British Crown. Rebel leaders were arrested and tried for treason, while some territories were subdued and others had their princely status restored or reaffirmed.

Bahadur Shah II was captured after the fall of Delhi. He was tried by the British and exiled to Rangoon in Burma. His death in 1862 marked the final end of the Mughal dynasty, which had once ruled much of the Indian subcontinent.

Despite its defeat, the Rebellion of 1857 (also referred to as the Sepoy Mutiny or the First War of Independence) remains one of the most significant events in India's history. It revealed the deep tensions that had developed under British rule and demonstrated, for the first time on a large scale, the possibility of organized resistance to colonial power.

Effects of the Mutiny

Politics and Government

The rebellion had exposed serious weaknesses in the EIC's administration and raised troubling questions in Britain about whether a commercial enterprise should continue ruling such a vast territory. India had become too important politically, economically, and strategically to remain under the authority of a private company. As a result, the British government stepped in and assumed direct control.

The British Parliament formalized this change by passing the Government of India Act of 1858. The act abolished the EIC's authority over India and transferred political power directly to the British Crown. Queen Victoria became the sovereign ruler of India, though she would only assume the formal title "Empress of India" in 1876 under the Royal Titles Act.

When Parliament passed the Government of India Act on August 2nd, 1858, it effectively transferred political and administrative control of India from the East India Company to the British government. To manage the country's administration, Parliament created the position of secretary of state for India, who would be responsible for overseeing Indian affairs from London.

The first person appointed to the position was Edward Stanley, 15th Earl of Derby, commonly known as Lord Stanley. His primary responsibility was to oversee the transition of power and supervise the governance of India on behalf of the British government.

At the same time, the position of governor-general of India was expanded. The governor-general now also carried the title of viceroy, acting as the Crown's direct representative in India. The first person to hold this dual role was Charles Canning, who had already been serving as governor-general during the rebellion.

Although the British had ultimately won the conflict, the rebellion had been a sobering wake-up call. Many British officials believed that some of the grievances that fueled the uprising had stemmed from the way India had been governed under East India Company rule. Indians had largely been excluded from political decision-making, and British authorities had often ignored local concerns.

In an effort to stabilize the country and prevent future uprisings, the British government sought to involve Indian elites more directly in the administration. As part of this policy, the Indian Councils Act of 1861 was passed, allowing Indians to sit on legislative councils for the first time.

Among the early Indian members were the Raja of Benaras, the Maharaja of Patiala, and Sir Dinkar Rao. These members were appointed rather than elected, and their powers were limited, but their inclusion marked a symbolic shift in colonial governance. For the first time, Indians were formally included in the legislative process, even if their influence was modest.

Other notable reforms followed. The British government abandoned Lord Dalhousie's Doctrine of Lapse, which had previously allowed the annexation of princely states that lacked a biological male heir. The policy had angered many Indian rulers and was widely seen as one of the grievances that contributed to the rebellion. By abandoning the doctrine, the British hoped to reassure Indian princes that their territories and dynasties would be respected as long as they remained loyal to the Crown.

As a result, princely states were allowed to retain a significant degree of internal autonomy, though they remained subordinate to British authority. This arrangement created a system of indirect rule that would become a defining feature of the British Raj.

The military also underwent major changes. Determined to prevent another large-scale uprising, the British reorganized the Indian Army. Greater emphasis was placed on recruiting soldiers from communities that British officials considered more loyal, such as Sikhs, Gurkhas, and Pathans. Recruitment from the Bengal sepoy regiments, many of whom had participated in the rebellion, was sharply reduced.

Regiments were deliberately composed of soldiers from different regions, castes, and religious groups in order to discourage unity and collective rebellion. At the same time, the number of European troops stationed in India was increased to strengthen British control.

These newly reorganized regiments would go on to serve the British Empire around the world, including in major conflicts such as the First and Second World Wars.

Society and the Economy

Socially, Britain tried to be more inclusive and respectful of traditional, religious practices and beliefs. However, it was nearly impossible to stop the "Westernization" of the country. Many of India's traditional structures and ways of life were slowly replaced by Western values and notions, creating a new class of Indians who were English-educated and imitated the British. They would go on to play a key role in the rise of India's nationalism, as we will discuss later.

Ending the rebellion proved to be an expensive undertaking. The cost of suppressing the uprising and restoring British authority placed a heavy financial burden on the Indian colonial administration. Much of this expense was ultimately borne by India itself, increasing pressure on the country's revenue system and placing additional strain on farmers who were required to meet land tax demands.

Agriculture remained the primary source of revenue for the colonial government, but it was not the only one. Income from the highly lucrative opium trade with China, along with taxes on commodities such as salt, cotton, and tea, also contributed significantly to the annual revenue collected by the British.

In an effort to stabilize the colonial budget, the British government introduced new financial measures, including a temporary income tax in 1860. Though intended as a short-term solution, the measure reflected the growing fiscal demands of maintaining the empire.

Meanwhile, the modernization of India's infrastructure, which had begun a decade earlier under Lord Dalhousie, continued to expand. The rapid growth of the railway network, in particular, transformed India's economic and social landscape. Railways allowed goods, people, and soldiers to move across vast distances with unprecedented speed, strengthening both trade and imperial control.

The extraction of India's resources continued under British rule. Colonial economic policies prioritized the needs of the empire, ensuring that India remained a major supplier of raw materials and a source of revenue within Britain's global trading system.

Very Brief Overview of the British Raj

After the EIC left and the British government came in to rule directly, India entered a new era. The period between 1858 and 1947 would become known as the British Raj. This period saw the modernization of India, particularly in education and infrastructure, though these changes were uneven and largely designed to serve imperial interests rather than the Indian population. It was also a time marked by social upheaval and continued exploitation of the Indian population by British colonial authorities.

Britain may have genuinely wanted to rule differently from the East India Company. Queen Victoria's Proclamation of 1858 set the tone, promising non-interference in religion, equal treatment under the law, the protection of princely states, and the inclusion of Indians in public service. On paper, it signaled a new era of fairer governance. However, the truth was that there could be no real change if Indians were not viewed as equals or partners. The handover of rule did not wipe away the racism or Britain's belief that, as white people, they were the superior race. Because of these opinions, they could never fully accept Indians as being on the same level as them.

In practice, the changes that followed 1857 were structural rather than meaningful. Aggressive annexation policies, such as the Doctrine of Lapse, were dropped, and greater reliance was placed on princely states to help govern. The army was reorganized along ethnic and regional lines to prevent future unity among soldiers. But in many ways, racial segregation between the British and Indians increased rather than decreased in the years following the rebellion.

The administration of India was run through the Indian Civil Service, which became the backbone of British governance. Civil service examinations were held in London, making it nearly impossible for most Indians to realistically enter. Power remained firmly in British hands, which was why the reforms of this era often felt superficial to those living under them.

Britain was also concerned about history repeating itself. If the Indians had risen up and revolted once, what would stop them from doing it again? Worried about anti-British sentiment and determined to prevent any future revolts, the British became more authoritarian and controlling, which had the exact opposite effect, fueling a greater desire for autonomy among the Indians.

Once the dust had settled after the rebellion, it quickly became apparent that the ousting of the EIC had been nothing but a band-aid solution. While the empire's stepping in had the immediate effect of sweeping the unrest and resentment against the EIC under the rug, it didn't actually solve any of the real issues or concerns faced by the Indians. Indians continued to be discriminated against. The costs of suppressing the rebellion had been charged back to Indian revenues, land taxes remained high, and the expanding railway network was built primarily to move troops and goods rather than to benefit ordinary

Indians. It is not surprising that beneath the surface, tensions continued to simmer slowly.

Lord Dalhousie

To understand why tensions had grown so severe by the 1850s, it is necessary to look at the policies of Lord Dalhousie. James Andrew Broun-Ramsay, the 1st Marquess of Dalhousie, was an important figure during the EIC's rule of India. He held the role of governor-general of India for nearly a decade, from 1848 to 1856.

His annexation policies and aggressive expansion plans helped to consolidate Britain's power and control over much of the subcontinent and contributed to the feelings of unrest and growing resentment within the Indian population.

However, he also implemented many Westernized policies in the country, which led to many important reforms in India. Whether this was good or bad, or even something the Indian people wanted, is difficult to state conclusively, but there is no doubt that he helped propel India into the modern era. Some of his most notable reforms included developing the communication and transportation industries. Under his guidance, the foundations of India's railway system were laid, with the first lines opening in 1853.

Portrait of James Broun-Ramsay, 1st Marquess of Dalhousie (1812–1860).[6]

Canals and irrigation systems were also expanded during this period, helping to increase agricultural production. Plantation agriculture for commodities such as tea and cotton grew steadily, reflecting the colonial government's interest in developing export-oriented crops. These policies were closely tied to Britain's economic interests and helped facilitate the trade and transportation of goods across the subcontinent.

Dalhousie also centralized the postal system in 1854, creating a more efficient national service, and supported educational reforms that expanded schooling, including initiatives encouraging education for girls.

Within his eight years in office, he significantly reshaped the political, social, and economic landscape of India. By the time he returned to Britain in 1856, India's administrative systems and transportation networks had begun to change dramatically.

While many of his achievements are often overshadowed by the controversial Doctrine of Lapse, Dalhousie played a major role in strengthening Britain's control over the subcontinent. His policies further integrated India into the British imperial economy and helped lay the foundations of the colonial system that would define the British Raj.

Chapter 3: An "Indian-dustrial" Revolution

Industrial Revolution in Britain

Beginning in 1760, Great Britain went through a major social change known as the Industrial Revolution, which lasted for approximately eighty years, until the mid-19th century.

Most people equate the Industrial Revolution with the invention of the Watt steam engine, and it is without a doubt one of the most significant inventions from this period, as it would go on to influence the invention of many other things, like ships, trains, and the production of goods. The steam engine's development was the work of several inventors over many decades. Thomas Savery built an early steam pump in 1698 to pump out flooded mine shafts, and this was followed by Thomas Newcomen's more practical atmospheric engine in 1712. It was James Watt, however, who transformed it into the powerful and efficient engine that would drive the Industrial Revolution forward. He patented his improvements in 1769.

By 1800, between 2,000 and 2,500 steam engines were scattered around factories and mills in Britain. This invention dramatically changed every aspect of British life. Suddenly, many labor-intensive tasks could be done using machines powered by steam engines, which, in turn, transformed other industries, like textiles and transportation.

The invention of the power loom machine, patented by Edmund Cartwright in 1785, significantly reduced the need for hand weaving.

Instead of employing dozens or hundreds of workers to produce cloth, the factory owner needed just a few. While the need for skilled workers declined sharply, the need for factory workers skyrocketed as factories started to be built.

Factory and manufacturing work led to unprecedented economic growth, as well as large-scale migration from rural areas to urban cities, as people sought new opportunities. Britain shifted from an agrarian country to an industrial one.

For many people, their quality of life also increased, as some products and goods became less expensive and easier to attain, though it is worth noting that early factory conditions were harsh, child labor was widespread, and urban overcrowding and disease were common realities for the working poor. Our present-day culture of mass consumption can be traced back to this time, as consumers suddenly had access to a wide range of products in a mass market.

Another interesting and life-altering invention that was made during the Industrial Revolution was the camera. Suddenly, portraits were no longer an upper-class luxury but something that could be accessible to nearly all classes. The camera also had a direct impact on art, as artists no longer felt the need to focus on capturing accuracy and felt free to pour emotion or subjectivity into their works.

The transportation industry was also forever changed with the invention of the steam engine. When railways were first introduced, they were mainly used to transport materials such as coal and silver. George Stephenson, the owner of a company that built railway trains, wondered if the same couldn't be done to transport people. Thus, Locomotion No. 1 was built, the first public steam railway to carry passengers. In September 1825, the train made its first journey carrying passengers in northern England on the Stockton and Darlington Railway, driven by George himself. This would just be the start; within decades, passenger trains would sprout up across Britain.

By the time the British Crown took direct rule of India in 1858, though British influence via the East India Company had already shaped the country for over a century, their technologies and modern inventions had advanced quite a bit. The British brought many of these inventions to India, leading to a period of significant industrialization.

India's Industrialization and Its Impact

While India's industrialization wasn't quite as extensive as Britain's, it was largely shaped by the empire's policies, and its effects, both positive and negative, were felt in nearly all aspects of Indian life, heavily influencing the people, the economy, and society.

This period of industrialization transformed the technology, communication, and transportation sectors in the country. The year 1854 is typically associated with the beginning of industrialization in India, marked by the opening of the country's first steam-powered cotton mill in Bombay.

Due to an increased and growing demand for goods like food and textiles from people both abroad and at home, it became clear to the British Empire that it would be impossible to keep up with demand simply through hand production methods. There was a real need to mass-produce, necessitating the creation of factories and machinery that could churn out goods in bulk.

India was rich in natural resources and minerals like cotton, iron, and coal, so it became central to the scaling of products like cotton, sugar, and paper. The abundance of resources and cheap labor lowered the costs and fueled the growth of industries, though it is worth noting that growth was uneven across regions. Also, many traditional industries declined.

A second mill, producing jute—a rough, raw fiber that is spun into fabric—followed suit. While the growth was slow, it was not long before more and more mills and factories producing items like sugar, paper, rubber, iron, and steel were thriving and popping up all over the country.

With the influx of goods, transportation became a pressing concern. Raw materials, factory workers, and finished goods all had to be transported across the country. In order to meet these demands, railways, canals, and roads were built. The railways, in particular, served multiple purposes for the empire, including transporting raw materials to ports for export, moving troops when needed, and strengthening Britain's trade networks. India eventually grew to have the fourth-largest rail network in the world.

The combination of all these factors marked the beginning of India's shift from a traditional, agriculture-based economy to a more industrialized one. And at the heart of this shift was the railway network.

India's Railways

One of the most transformative legacies of British rule on the country was the railway system. It was first proposed in 1832 to serve industrial needs. At that point, rail travel was still a very new concept in Britain; however, the EIC had a vision of how beneficial a network of railways could be in India and went about developing a system. Construction of a railway track in Madras between Red Hills and Chintadripet began in 1835, with the line ready for operations in 1837. England shipped a rotary steam engine, and the track began to be used to transport granite. Additional lines were built to transport construction materials and supplies.

In 1845, the East Indian Railway Company was established, followed by the Great Indian Peninsula Railway in 1849. By 1853, India's first passenger railway line had been completed and was ready for service. The inaugural journey, carrying about four hundred passengers in fourteen carriages, took place on April 16th, 1853, covering a distance of thirty-four kilometers (twenty-one miles) between Bori Bunder in Bombay and Thane.

Above : The first railway train on the East Indian Railway. (Reproduced by courtesy of 'The Illustrated London News').

The first train of the East Indian Railway, 1854.[7]

Following this first successful trip, railway construction expanded rapidly across eastern and southern India. Lines were opened around Calcutta and Madras, and the network steadily pushed inland. By 1864, a through railway connection linked Calcutta with Delhi, creating one of the first major trunk routes (major transportation lines) across northern India. A few years later, the Allahabad–Jabalpur line was completed in 1870, linking the East Indian Railway with the Great Indian Peninsula Railway and creating the first continuous rail route between Calcutta and Bombay. By the late 1860s, these expanding lines formed a growing network spanning roughly four thousand miles.

During the 1840s and 1850s, several railway companies were established to build railway lines across India, and construction accelerated in the years that followed. After the Rebellion of 1857, the East India Company was removed from power, and the British Crown assumed direct rule of India. The British government began to play a larger role in overseeing railway expansion, though private companies remained responsible for building and operating many of the lines.

To encourage private investors to finance railway construction, the British government guaranteed railway companies a fixed return on their investments. If the railways did not make enough profit, the difference was paid from Indian revenues. This policy helped the railway network expand rapidly, but it also meant that much of the financial risk was carried by India itself.

By 1880, roughly nine thousand miles of railway track had been laid across the country. These lines linked Bombay, Madras, and Calcutta—the three major port cities of British India—and formed the backbone of the growing railway system.

Over the following decades, trains continued to improve, and new lines were built across the subcontinent. Basic amenities such as toilets gradually began appearing on trains, making long journeys more manageable for passengers. By 1895, India was even building some of its own locomotives. Indian laborers were also recruited by the British to work on railway construction projects in other parts of the empire, particularly on the Uganda Railway in East Africa.

In the early 20ᵗʰ century, the administration of the railways was reorganized. The Railway Board was established in 1905 to improve the management of the rapidly growing system. Around this time, the government also began purchasing some of the major railway lines from private companies and leasing them back for operation.

The outbreak of World War I slowed railway expansion considerably. Britain diverted many of its resources and manpower to the war effort in Europe, and the railway system in India began to suffer from neglect and overuse. By the end of the war, many parts of the network were in poor condition.

Reforms were introduced in the years that followed, and in 1924, the government created a separate railway budget to better manage railway finances. In the decades that followed, the railway network in India continued to expand while train technology steadily improved.

The impact of railways on India was profound. The network reshaped the country's political, social, and economic landscape.

Socially, railways helped connect the people of a vast and diverse country. Travel became easier and faster, allowing people to move greater distances than before. New opportunities for employment and education emerged, as people were no longer confined to the places where they were born.

Economically, railways helped transport raw materials, boosted trade and production, and made it easier to move manufactured goods across the country. The growing demand for goods contributed to industrial development and created new employment opportunities. Over time, this also encouraged migration from rural areas to larger cities, gradually changing population patterns and ways of life.

Today, India's railway network spans roughly 68,000 kilometers (42,000 miles) of route length with more than 100,000 kilometers (62,000 miles) of total track. It remains one of the largest railway systems in the world, ranking fourth globally behind the United States, China, and Russia.

De-industrialization: The Cost of Modernization

As we can see, the Industrial Revolution brought about many changes in India. Sadly, many of these developments were designed primarily to serve British interests by making the extraction and transportation of resources more efficient and cost-effective. The modernization of India was often an unintended by-product rather than the main goal.

The flip side of the Industrial Revolution is the concept of "de-industrialization," which argues that Britain's rule in India and the empire's economic policies had damaging effects on India's traditional industries and economy.

Before Britain gained political control in the mid-18th century, India had numerous well-developed and flourishing industries. The country was especially famous for its textiles, exporting cotton cloth, silk, and fine muslin to markets across Europe, the Middle East, and Asia. India also produced pottery, jewelry, metal goods, and ships. Iron and steel were manufactured for tools, weapons, and other uses.

Some economic historians estimate that around 1750, India accounted for roughly 20 to 25 percent of the world's manufacturing output, much of it coming from the textile industry. India's reputation for high-quality goods was one of the reasons European trading companies became so interested in the region. Under East India

Company rule and later during the British Raj, a growing share of textile manufacturing shifted to Britain, severely undermining many traditional industries in India.

While technological advances and factory production made things more productive, they also had serious social and economic consequences. Factory-made goods were far cheaper to produce than handmade ones, and the influx of machine-made textiles into Indian markets reduced demand for locally produced cloth. As a result, many artisans lost their livelihoods, and numerous traditional crafts declined.

Women were particularly affected. Many had supported themselves or their families by spinning cotton, preparing yarn, and embroidering and sewing. The spread of machine-spun yarn and factory-produced textiles disrupted these sources of income and contributed to the de-industrialization of rural household industries.

India's economy also became increasingly tied to British policies and priorities. British tariff policies often favored British manufacturers, allowing British goods to enter Indian markets more easily while making it harder for Indian industries to compete.

Decades of exporting raw materials and transferring wealth abroad also strained India's economy. Many Indian thinkers later argued that colonial trade policies drained wealth from the country, leaving it poorer despite its vast resources.

Workers' Conditions

Earlier in Britain's history, it had profited enormously from the transatlantic slave trade. In India, however, wealth was extracted primarily through unequal trade policies and the labor of colonial workers.

Many of Britain's modernization projects depended on large numbers of Indian laborers. Hundreds of thousands of workers were employed building railways, roads, and canals. They worked in textile mills, factories, plantations, and mines. These workers often endured long hours, low wages, and difficult conditions as the colonial economy expanded.

Working Environment and Wages

Working conditions in Indian factories and many other industries were often harsh, unsanitary, and dangerous. Workers were expected to endure long hours—often twelve to fourteen hours a day—and the wages they received were usually barely enough to support their families.

In the early decades of industrialization, there were few laws that effectively regulated wages or working conditions. Workers in different industries received different levels of pay, and women were typically paid less than men. Skilled workers, such as carpenters, mechanics, or railway artisans (specialists who repaired trains), often earned more than laborers employed in textile mills or other factories.

Employers generally managed their workforce in a strict and authoritarian manner. Discipline could include fines, wage deductions, or dismissal for mistakes or poor performance.

The factories and worksites themselves were often unsafe. Ventilation was poor, machinery was crowded together, and safety measures were minimal. Workers frequently spent long hours in dusty, overheated environments that contributed to respiratory illnesses, such as tuberculosis and other lung diseases.

Accidents were common. Workers could lose limbs in machinery or suffer serious injuries due to unsafe equipment and overcrowded conditions. At the same time, rapid industrial growth and crowded urban living conditions contributed to the spread of diseases such as cholera and plague in many industrial cities.

Working in mines was often even more dangerous. Miners labored deep underground in poorly ventilated tunnels and were frequently exposed to dust, toxic gases, and unstable rock formations. Accidents such as tunnel collapses, flooding, and gas explosions could be deadly.

For many laborers, injuries or illness meant losing their only source of income. Without strong legal protections or social safety systems, families who depended on these wages could quickly fall deeper into poverty.

Women and Children

The majority of Indians working in factories, mines, and other industries were men, but women and children also worked in factories, fields, plantations, and mines. Young girls were employed in British households as ayahs, nannies or nursemaids. They often helped raise the children of colonial families. While these jobs came with their own difficulties, they could sometimes offer more stable conditions than the demanding labor found in the factories or fields.

For employers, women and children were a cheaper source of labor because they were paid lower wages than men.

In some industries, children were employed to perform tasks such as sorting fibers, carrying materials, or assisting with machinery. In the mining industry, women and children were often employed to carry minerals such as coal or ore. The work was physically demanding and took place in dangerous environments. Over time, growing concerns about safety led to laws that gradually restricted the employment of women and children in underground mining.

Industrial and plantation labor could also expose workers to harsh conditions, long hours, and health risks. In some sectors, particularly plantations and domestic service, women and children were vulnerable to exploitation and abuse.

Debt Bondage

Debt bondage was a widespread practice in many parts of colonial India. It often occurred when a worker struggling to survive borrowed money from a landlord, moneylender, or employer. In return, the borrower was expected to repay the debt through labor or by surrendering a portion of their wages.

In theory, the arrangement appeared simple, but in practice, it often trapped workers in long-term contracts. Lenders frequently charged extremely high interest rates, which could quickly inflate the original debt. As a result, many laborers found it nearly impossible to repay what they owed. In some cases, debts were carried over to the next generation, trapping entire families in cycles of poverty and obligation.

Colonial labor systems and weak regulatory protections allowed forms of bonded labor to persist in several sectors, particularly in agriculture, plantations, and some rural industries. Because employers benefited from having a stable and inexpensive labor force, the system could be difficult for workers to escape.

Although various laws were later introduced to restrict these exploitative labor practices, bonded labor and similar systems continued to exist in parts of India. The legacy of these practices can still be seen in some rural areas today.

India would likely have experienced modernization over time as global economies evolved. However, some scholars suggest that without colonial rule, the process of modernization might have developed differently, possibly allowing India to retain greater control over its resources and industries.

Chapter 4: A "Great" Famine and Even Greater Consequences

As the pressure from Britain's colonial policies and the negative impacts of industrialization continued to ripple across India, an intense drought swept over the country. New challenges surfaced, plunging the country into a humanitarian crisis.

The drought would later be viewed as the straw that broke the camel's back, becoming the catalyst for a devastating famine that would soon sweep the nation, mainly affecting the southern and western parts of India and claiming the lives of the most vulnerable in society.

Roughly six to ten million people died during the famine. In the rural parts of the country, whole villages and communities were wiped out. Those who escaped death suffered in other ways. They lost their homes, land, and other material possessions. They suffered from starvation, diseases, and complications related to malnutrition.

By the time the famine had swept through the country, very few lives had remained untouched or unscarred. The famine disproportionately affected the rural poor and landless laborers, while elites were comparatively insulated.

Causes of the Great Famine of India

No single issue or event caused the Great Famine of 1876-78. Instead, the deadly famine, also known as the Southern India famine or the Madras famine, was caused by a combination of natural causes, British colonial policies, and existing social and economic hardship.

Mother Nature

The monsoon, a seasonal weather pattern that brings alternating wet and dry periods across India, is often seen as the country's lifeline. It plays a vital role in nearly every aspect of life, especially agriculture.

In the summer, the monsoon brings heavy rainfall that fills wells, waters the soil, and feeds lakes and rivers. This rain provides life-sustaining water for villages, farms, and livestock. It is especially important in regions that lack irrigation systems or reliable water sources.

India's agricultural industry has long been heavily dependent on the summer monsoon. The success or failure of the rains can mean the difference between a good harvest and a disastrous one. When rainfall is weak or fails, the effects ripple through the economy. Food becomes scarce, prices rise, and rural communities suffer the most.

Too much rain can also cause destruction. Floods can wipe out crops and damage towns and villages. For India's agricultural system to function well, a delicate balance between drought and flooding must be maintained each year.

In 1876, the summer monsoon failed across large parts of the country. Many regions faced a prolonged and devastating drought. Modern research has linked this drought to a powerful El Niño climate event that disrupted weather patterns across the globe. During the same period, severe droughts also struck China, Brazil, and parts of Africa.

Without rainfall and with little irrigation available, crops failed, which led to a severe food shortage. Farmers who were already struggling suddenly had no crops to sell, no food to feed their families, and no way to pay the taxes demanded by the colonial government.

Industrialization and British Exploitation

It is likely that the suffering of the Indians could have been reduced if colonial policies had been different. The famine was triggered by drought, but many historians argue that British policies made the disaster far worse.

Famines were not new to India, but the colonial era saw several devastating ones. The Great Famine of 1876–78 was only one of a series of major famines that struck the subcontinent during British rule. However, as famine spread, colonial authorities often continued prioritizing trade and revenue collection.

The demand for raw materials had already begun reshaping India's agricultural landscape. In many regions, farmers were encouraged to grow cash crops such as cotton, tea, and indigo for export. While food crops were still grown, the increasing focus on export agriculture left some areas more vulnerable when drought struck.

During the famine, grain continued to be exported from parts of India to international markets. The railways could move food quickly across the country, but distribution was often shaped by market needs rather than relief needs.

Land revenue demands also remained high. Although some relief measures were eventually introduced, many people were still expected to pay taxes despite their poor harvests. In order to survive, families were often forced to sell land, homes, livestock, or other possessions.

Existing Social and Economic Problems

Long-standing social and economic inequalities in India also made the famine more deadly. Much of the population depended on agriculture for survival. When crops failed, farmers lost both their food supply and their source of income. Artisans who had already been affected by industrial changes often had few alternatives for earning a living.

The poorest members of society—landless laborers, small farmers, and rural workers—were the most vulnerable. Without savings, land, or resources to fall back on, many families had little chance of surviving a prolonged drought.

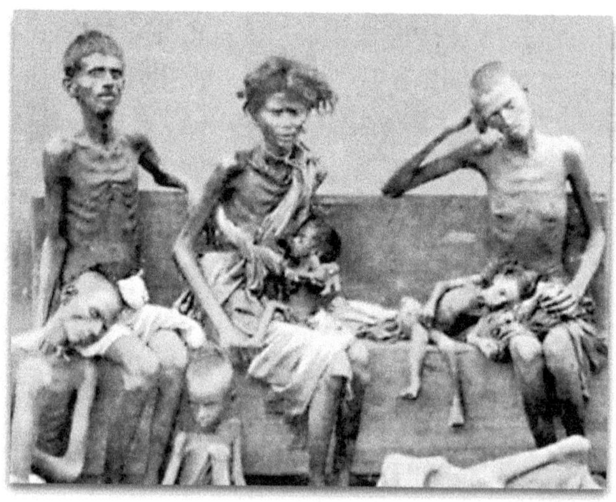

A family in India during the Great Famine, 1877.[8]

Artisans who had once supported themselves through traditional crafts such as weaving or pottery had already begun losing their livelihoods due to industrial changes. Many had been forced into farming or wage labor, leaving them vulnerable when the harvests failed.

The deep inequalities within Indian society also shaped who survived and who did not. Those with land, wealth, or resources were often better able to endure the crisis, while the rural poor suffered the most.

Britain's Response to the Famine

Looking back on how the British responded to the famine, most historians agree that their response was not only inadequate but likely made the situation worse and resulted in a significantly higher number of deaths.

Even when faced with the devastating humanitarian crisis, Britain's primary focus remained on exploiting the country and advancing the empire's interests. Heading the Crown's interests was Lord Lytton, the man who served as viceroy of India from 1876 to 1880.

Lord Lytton

The 1st Earl of Lytton is closely associated with the Great Famine, which started soon after he arrived in India.

Edward Robert Bulwer-Lytton was born in England into a prominent literary and political family; his father was the well-known Victorian novelist and politician Edward Bulwer-Lytton. He entered diplomatic service as a teenager and spent years serving in various diplomatic posts across Europe and the United States. Through these assignments, he steadily rose through the ranks and eventually caught the attention of the British government. In 1876, he was appointed viceroy of India.

Lord Lytton.[9]

Only a few months after arriving in India, on January 1ˢᵗ, 1877, Lytton organized the Delhi Durbar, also known as the Proclamation Durbar. The ceremony was intended to celebrate Queen Victoria's new title as "Empress of India."

The gathering was a grand display of imperial power and prestige. Tens of thousands of people were present in and around Delhi for the occasion, including British officials and Indian rulers who had set up elaborate camps outside the city. They were there to formally recognize Victoria's imperial authority and pledge loyalty to the Crown.

However, to many observers, the celebration appeared deeply insensitive. While this lavish event was taking place, large parts of India were already suffering from the devastating famine. Critics later argued that the resources and attention devoted to the ceremony could have been better used to address the growing humanitarian crisis. The Delhi Durbar became a symbol of the disconnect between colonial authorities and the suffering population.

Lytton's tenure as viceroy remains controversial. His administration was marked by policies that many historians argue prioritized imperial interests and economic stability over the welfare of the Indian population.

One of the most debated aspects of his rule during the Great Famine was the government's reliance on laissez-faire economic ideas. This approach emphasized minimal interference in markets and limited government intervention.

Because of this policy, British officials were hesitant to interfere heavily in the grain trade or impose strict controls on prices and distribution. Relief measures were introduced, but they were often tightly controlled and widely criticized as inadequate.

Relief camps and public works projects were established where famine victims could work in exchange for food or wages. However, the wages offered were extremely low. Some historians have described them as falling short of the level needed to adequately sustain workers, meaning laborers often remained weak and malnourished even while participating in relief work.

Many British officials feared that large-scale food distribution or generous financial relief would create dependency and discourage people from working. Others believed that government interference in markets could disrupt trade and worsen economic conditions.

These ideas shaped the government's response to the famine, and they remain the subject of significant historical debate to this day. Critics argue that stricter intervention, greater relief spending, and earlier action might have reduced the scale of the tragedy.

Consequences and Legacy of the Famine

Famines were nothing new in India. During the 18th, 19th, and early 20th centuries, different parts of the country periodically suffered devastating food shortages. Some notable examples include the Bengal Famine of 1770, the Bengal Famine of 1943, the Chalisa Famine of 1783–1784, and the Odisha Famine of 1866. These disasters often occurred when drought, crop failures, and widespread poverty combined to leave large numbers of people unable to access enough food.

One reason the Great Famine of 1876–78 stands out is the sheer number of lives that were lost and the political consequences that followed. The British government's response to the famine drew heavy criticism in both India and Britain. For many people, the disaster exposed the darker side of colonial rule and strengthened growing resentment toward British authority.

Faced with a staggering death toll and mounting criticism, the British government began to take steps to show that it was addressing the problem. Officials also feared that widespread anger among the population could lead to further unrest or even another rebellion.

In response, Britain established the Indian Famine Commission in 1880. The commission was tasked with studying the causes of the famine and recommending ways to deal with future food crises. Based on its findings, famine codes were gradually introduced in the early 1880s. These guidelines created procedures for identifying famine conditions and organizing relief efforts when food shortages occurred.

Under the administration of the new viceroy, Lord Ripon, these policies began shaping how the colonial government responded to future famines.

Lord Ripon

The new viceroy who took office in 1880 was very different from Lord Lytton. His manner of governing and his attitude toward Indians contrasted sharply with that of his predecessor.

Named George Frederick Samuel Robinson, Lord Ripon was the second son of British Prime Minister Frederick John Robinson. Born into a prominent political family, Ripon spent much of his career in public service. Over the years, he held several important government positions in Britain, including serving as under-secretary and later secretary of state for India.

By the time he was appointed viceroy, Ripon already had experience dealing with Indian affairs. When he arrived in India, he had a reputation as a liberal-minded reformer. He hoped to introduce policies to improve colonial administration.

After Lord Lytton's controversial rule, Ripon represented a noticeable change in tone. His policies were generally more sympathetic toward Indian concerns, and he gained the respect of many educated Indians and early reformers. He introduced several reforms, supported greater local self-government, and expanded the powers of municipal councils and local governing bodies.

Ripon also backed the Ilbert Bill, which aimed to allow Indian judges to try European defendants in criminal cases. The proposal sparked fierce resistance from the European community in India, many of whom strongly opposed being tried in court by Indian judges. The controversy became one of the most heated political debates of the colonial period. When the bill was finally passed in a modified form in 1884, many of its original provisions had been weakened.

Ripon repealed the Vernacular Press Act of 1878, which had restricted the freedom of Indian-language newspapers. He also

Lord Ripon.[10]

established the Education Commission to review the state of education in India and recommend improvements to the system.

When Ripon's term as viceroy came to an end, he left behind a reputation as one of the more reform-minded administrators of the British Raj. Many Indians admired him for attempting to expand their participation in government and for challenging policies they believed were unfair.

Even today, buildings, roads, and institutions across India and Pakistan still bear his name, reflecting the respect he earned during his time in office.

Famine Code of 1883

As mentioned earlier, following the findings of the 1880 Famine Commission, famine codes were introduced in the early 1880s during Lord Ripon's administration. These codes categorized different stages of food shortages, such as near-scarcity, scarcity, and full famine.

The goal of the famine codes was to create a clearer plan for how the government should respond to food shortages. They outlined the steps officials should take to prevent famine where possible and the relief measures that should be introduced if famine could not be avoided.

The codes encouraged closer monitoring of rainfall, crop conditions, and food prices so that shortages could be identified earlier. They also recommended using railways, canals, and roads to move food and essential supplies into affected regions. Relief programs, such as public works employment, food distribution, and financial assistance, were also included.

Although the famine codes were an important step, they were far from perfect. The rules were not always followed in every region, and relief efforts often depended on the decisions of local officials.

At the same time, many Indians were becoming increasingly aware of the inequalities within colonial rule. The controversy surrounding the Ilbert Bill showed many Indians that Europeans were unwilling to treat them as equals under the law.

These events helped increase political awareness among educated Indians. Just a few years later, in 1885, the Indian National Congress was founded. The organization would eventually become one of the most important forces in India's struggle for self-government.

Chapter 5: Congress, Violence, and Social Movements

India's Social Structure: Caste System

Britain's rule in India led to another important change in the country's social fabric: the rise of a new middle class.

This did not happen overnight. It grew slowly as India changed under colonial rule. New schools opened, and new jobs appeared in government offices, courts, and businesses. Railways, printing presses, and trade expanded. All of this helped create a new group of educated professionals. And this group became what we now call the Indian middle class.

Before British rule, India did not have a middle class in the modern Western sense. However, that does not mean society was made up only of rulers and peasants. There were also wealthy merchants, traders, bankers, court officials, and administrators. These groups held influence and wealth, and in many ways, they formed a middle layer in society.

What colonial rule did was expand and reshape this layer. Western education, new professions, and government service created a larger class of lawyers, teachers, clerks, journalists, and civil servants.

To understand how this new class emerged, it helps to understand how Indian society was already organized. For centuries, much of Indian society had been structured around the caste system. According to traditional Hindu belief, society was divided into four broad groups known as varnas.

- Brahmins were the priests, scholars, and teachers. Religious texts described them as having come from the head of the creator god Brahma.
- Kshatriyas were the warriors and rulers, said to have come from Brahma's arms.
- Vaishyas were traders, merchants, and farmers, believed to have come from Brahma's thighs.
- Shudras were laborers and service workers, said to have come from Brahma's feet.

In reality, society was far more complex than these four groups suggest. Within them existed thousands of smaller communities known as castes, or jatis. By some estimates, there were around three thousand castes and more than twenty-five thousand sub-castes across the subcontinent.

Outside this hierarchy were communities later known as Dalits, who were historically treated as "untouchables" and faced severe discrimination.

Indian Caste System

India's caste system.[11]

One's caste shaped many parts of daily life. It influenced what work a person did, who they married, where they lived, and even who they could share food with. In many places, people mostly socialized and married within their own caste group.

Still, the system was not always as fixed as it might appear. Wealth, political power, and regional customs sometimes allowed groups to rise or change their social standing over time.

When the British arrived, they encountered this complex social structure and tried to organize it in ways that made administration easier. Beginning with the census of 1871, colonial officials started classifying and recording castes across India. These surveys attempted to place communities into neat categories and rankings. Over time, this process helped make caste identities more rigid. Groups that had once been flexible or locally defined were now written down and officially recorded.

Colonial policies sometimes reinforced these divisions. Certain communities were favored for government jobs or recruited into the colonial army under the British idea of "martial races," the belief that certain ethnic groups were naturally better soldiers than others.

The Middle Class

Since India experienced a series of major historical changes, it is only natural that Indian society began to transform. One of the most important developments was the emergence of a new middle class.

In Europe, the rise of the middle class was closely tied to industrialization. As factories expanded, new jobs appeared for managers, professionals, and merchants. Industrialization played a role in India as well, but the story there was somewhat different. The growth of India's middle class was shaped just as much by Britain's colonial policies and style of rule.

First, let's consider the effects of industrialization. As we saw in earlier chapters, industrialization introduced new industries and helped cities grow. Even so, India remained largely agrarian during this period. Most people still lived in villages and worked the land.

However, factories and workshops did create new opportunities. People from rural communities began moving to large cities such as Bombay and Calcutta in search of work. As factories produced more goods, trade expanded, and ports became busier. This created jobs in shipping, transport, and commerce.

Cities had to adapt as well. As more people arrived, small businesses began appearing everywhere. Shops, food stalls, and restaurants opened to serve the growing workforce.

Slowly, a new social structure began to appear alongside the traditional caste system. At the bottom were laborers who worked long hours in factories, fields, and construction. At the top were wealthy industrialists, merchants, and large landowners.

Between them, a new class began to form. This group included teachers, doctors, lawyers, engineers, clerks, and civil servants. Many of them had received a Western-style education and spoke English. They worked in offices, schools, courts, and government departments rather than in fields or factories.

They earned more than laborers but far less than the wealthy elite. What set them apart was not simply money but also their education and profession.

This was the beginning of India's modern middle class. It is important to note that not everyone with wealth was considered part of the middle class. Education mattered most. A trader might become rich, but without formal schooling, he would not necessarily be seen as middle class in the same way as a lawyer, teacher, or civil servant.

This is where British influence had its greatest impact. A turning point came in 1835 when British politician Thomas Babington Macaulay presented his famous "Minute on Education." It argued that English should become the language of higher education in India. Macaulay said he hoped to create a class of Indians who were "Indian in blood and colour, but English in tastes, opinions, morals and intellect."[1]

Whatever his intentions, the policy had lasting consequences. British authorities expanded schools, colleges, and universities across the country. These institutions taught subjects such as science, law, and history, often in English.

For the first time, large numbers of Indians began receiving modern university educations. Some even traveled to Britain to study and later returned home with new ideas about politics and society.

---

[1] Dr. Murali Mohan Krishna Prayaga. "Why Macaulay's Project Still Undermines India Today." https://etedge-insights.com/industry/education/why-macaulays-project-still-undermines-india-today

New technologies also helped connect the country. Railways, the telegraph, and a growing newspaper industry allowed ideas to travel quickly across vast distances. These newspapers and journals carried debates about reform, freedom, and self-government into homes, coffee houses, and university halls. The emerging middle class began to see itself as a group with shared interests and ambitions.

Many members of this class worked for the colonial administration. Others became teachers, journalists, lawyers, or doctors. As cities grew, there was a demand for accountants, clerks, bankers, engineers, and architects. These positions were often filled by English-educated Indians.

In many ways, this group stood between two worlds. On one side were older traditions and social hierarchies. On the other was a new, modern, and increasingly global outlook.

A number of important social reformers emerged during this period.

One of the earliest was Raja Ram Mohan Roy. In the early 19th century, he campaigned against the practice of sati, where widows were expected to die on their husband's funeral pyre. He also argued strongly for women's education.

Dadabhai Naoroji developed what became known as the Drain Theory, the argument that Britain was systematically extracting wealth from India and transferring it to Britain. According to this idea, colonial rule was not simply political domination. It was an economic system that steadily drained India's resources and left the country poorer over time. This theory gave the growing nationalist movement a powerful economic argument to support its political demands.

Another influential reformer was Ishwar Chandra Vidyasagar, who helped push for laws allowing Hindu widows to remarry and worked to expand education. Later reformers, such as Jyotirao Phule, challenged caste discrimination and fought to open schools for lower-caste communities and women.

In the 20th century, perhaps the strongest critic of caste inequality was B. R. Ambedkar. Born into a Dalit family, he rose to become a scholar, lawyer, and political leader. He later played a central role in writing India's constitution.

B. R. Ambedkar.[13]

These reformers were part of the same educated class that had begun to grow under colonial rule. Many of them believed India needed social reform just as much as political change.

For a time, this new middle class may even have seemed useful to the British authorities. They were educated, English-speaking, and often worked within the colonial system itself. However, that did not last.

No matter how modernized India became, one fact remained impossible to ignore: it was still a colonized country ruled by a foreign power. Both sides knew it. And as the British tried to tighten their control, tensions only continued to grow.

Nationalism in India

For decades, many Indians had felt unhappy, oppressed, and mistreated. Protests and small uprisings occurred from time to time, but they were usually suppressed by the colonial authorities. Uniting these factions across such a vast and diverse country seemed almost impossible.

Many Indians watched with growing frustration as colonial economic policies directed wealth and resources toward the British Empire. Raw materials flowed out of India while profits flowed back to Britain. Meanwhile, large parts of the Indian population continued to live in deep poverty.

The situation became even more painful during periods of famine. During several devastating famines in the late 19th century, millions of Indians died. Critics accused the colonial government of responding too slowly and prioritizing economic policy over human suffering.

For many Indians, these experiences made it clear that something had to change. And in an ironic twist, the very group Britain had helped create would soon become one of its strongest critics.

Through English-language schools and universities, Britain had educated a new class of Indians. These men were exposed to Western ideas about liberty, representation, and democracy. Over time, many began asking uncomfortable questions. Why should India be ruled by Britain? Who had given a foreign power the right to govern millions of Indians?

Events such as the controversy surrounding the Ilbert Bill further inflamed tensions. When British residents fiercely opposed the proposal allowing Indian judges to try European defendants, many Indians saw it as clear evidence of racial inequality under colonial rule.

Educated Indians began demanding a greater voice in government. With the encouragement of retired civil servant Allan Octavian Hume, they took the first steps toward organized political action, which eventually led to the formation of the Indian National Congress in 1885.

Allan Octavian Hume

Allan Octavian Hume was a writer, reformer, and naturalist who had spent many years working in India as a member of the Indian Civil Service. During his time in the country, he developed a deep interest in India and its people.

Hume believed Indians deserved a greater role in governing their own country. He was often critical of British policies and felt that India was sometimes poorly administered.

While serving as the collector (chief district administrator) of Etawah, he tried to improve the lives of people there. He introduced several reforms and worked to expand education.

Education became one of his main priorities. Hume helped open hundreds of village schools and strongly supported education for girls. He established free primary schooling in many areas, built a high school with his own money, and created scholarships to help students pursue higher education.

Hume also spoke out against social problems such as female infanticide and the harsh treatment of widows. During his time in Etawah, he helped start Hindi and Urdu language publications that gained popularity among local readers. In many ways, Hume believed that education and social reform would help prepare India for a more modern future.

Allan Octavian Hume.[18]

Later, he rose to become secretary of the Department of Revenue, Agriculture, and Commerce in India. But still, Hume did not hesitate to criticize colonial policies. He openly disagreed with the policies of Lord Lytton, whose administration many critics believed treated Indians unfairly.

After falling out with the government, Hume eventually retired from the civil service. He still continued to take a strong interest in India's political future.

Hume believed that growing frustration among Indians could eventually lead to another major uprising. He felt the country needed a national organization where educated Indians could express their concerns peacefully. In 1883, he wrote an open letter to the graduates of the University of Calcutta, urging them to come together and form such an organization.

Over the next few years, he contacted leading Indian intellectuals and political figures. With the encouragement of Lord Dufferin, Viceroy of India, plans were made for a national meeting.

The first gathering took place in December 1885 in Bombay. Seventy-two delegates attended the meeting. Most were lawyers, journalists, or other educated professionals representing different regions of India. At that meeting, the Indian National Congress was formally established.

What began as a small meeting of educated elites would eventually grow into the central political organization leading India's struggle for independence.

Indian National Congress

First session of the Indian National Congress, December 1885.[14]

The initial goal of the Indian National Congress was to bring together educated Indians who had been exposed to Western education and political ideas. The hope was that these individuals could work together to press the British government for reforms and greater Indian participation in governing the country.

Many British officials believed that if the organization was made up of English-educated Indians, its members would be willing to work within the existing colonial system. To some extent, especially in its early years, this proved true.

Many of the early leaders of the Indian National Congress believed strongly in ideas like liberty, equality, and the rule of law. They argued that Indians deserved the same rights and dignity as British citizens.

During its early years, the Indian National Congress worked cautiously and cooperatively with the British authorities. Its leaders preferred petitions, debates, and constitutional reform rather than confrontation. They hoped that gradual change would expand political participation and give Indians a greater voice in government.

In many ways, the early Indian National Congress resembled a gathering of educated elites rather than a mass political movement. Its members often came from privileged backgrounds and had more in common socially with British administrators than with the rural masses of India.

However, over time, this began to change. As the realities of colonial rule became clearer, some leaders began questioning whether British rule could ever truly be fair. How could ideas like liberty, equality, and justice exist in a country that remained under foreign control?

These questions gradually created divisions within the Indian National Congress. By the early 20th century, two distinct factions had emerged.

One group, known as the Moderates, believed reforms could still be achieved through cooperation with the British government. Leaders such as Gopal Krishna Gokhale supported gradual change through constitutional methods. They hoped India could eventually gain self-government within the British Empire.

The other faction believed a more assertive approach was necessary. Leaders such as Bal Gangadhar Tilak, Bipin Chandra Pal, and Lala Lajpat Rai (often called Lal, Bal, and Pal) argued that India needed stronger resistance to colonial rule. They promoted mass political participation, boycotts of British goods, and the revival of Indian pride in culture and history. Their goal was swaraj, or self-rule.

Tensions between these two factions continued to grow, especially after the controversial Partition of Bengal and the Swadeshi movement that followed. The conflict finally erupted during the Indian National Congress session in Surat in December 1907. The meeting quickly descended into chaos, with delegates shouting, throwing chairs, and even hurling shoes at one another. The event, known as the Surat Split, formally divided the Indian National Congress into Moderate and Radical factions.

The split lasted nearly a decade. In 1916, the two sides finally reunited at the Indian National Congress session in Lucknow. They had once again been united by the growing demand for greater self-government and an end to British domination.

Partition of Bengal (1905)

Sensing a growing wave of anger toward British rule and a rising sense of national unity, the British administration began looking for ways to weaken the movement. One method that had often worked in the past was to govern large and diverse populations by balancing different regions, communities, and interests against each other.

Bengal soon became the focus of their attention. At the time, Bengal was one of the largest and most politically active provinces in British India. It had a population of nearly eighty million people and was widely seen as the center of the growing nationalist movement. Bengali leaders within the Indian National Congress were especially vocal in pushing for political reform.

Officially, the British government argued that Bengal was simply too large to govern efficiently. Dividing the province, they claimed, would make administration easier and improve governance.

So, in 1905, under the authority of Lord Curzon, the province of Bengal was divided into two new territories. The western portion, which included Calcutta, remained largely Hindu-majority. The eastern region became the new province of Eastern Bengal and Assam, where Muslims formed the majority. Both provinces still contained large religious minorities, but the division created two regions with different demographics.

To understand why this decision was so controversial, it is important to understand the relationship between Hindus and Muslims in India. For centuries, the two communities had lived alongside each other. Their history included periods of tension and conflict, but there were also long stretches of cooperation and shared daily life. Markets, towns, and villages were often home to both communities.

Muslim rulers during the Mughal period varied in their approach to religion. Some, like Akbar, were known for policies of tolerance and inclusion. Others, such as Aurangzeb, took a more orthodox religious stance. Despite these differences, everyday life for many people often crossed religious boundaries.

When the British expanded their rule in India, both Hindus and Muslims sometimes found themselves united in opposition to foreign authority. During the Rebellion of 1857, soldiers and civilians from both communities participated in the uprising against the British. When the British eventually suppressed the uprising, they became concerned about the possibility of united resistance in the future.

Over time, colonial policies increasingly categorized Indians by religion and community in administrative and political contexts. This gradually encouraged people to think of themselves as members of separate political groups.

It was in this atmosphere that the partition of Bengal took place. To many Indian nationalists, the decision looked like a deliberate attempt to weaken the growing nationalist movement by dividing the population.

Instead of calming tensions, the decision triggered a wave of anger across the country. Many Indians saw the partition as an insult and an attack on Bengali identity. Protests erupted across Bengal and quickly spread to other parts of India.

Out of this anger grew the Swadeshi movement. Indians began boycotting British goods and encouraging the use of locally made products instead. The movement also promoted Indian industry, education, and cultural pride.

Swadeshi Movement

The idea behind the Swadeshi movement was simple. If the British ruled India through economic power, then Indians could resist by withdrawing their support from British goods.

One of the movement's main strategies was a boycott of British products. Across Bengal and other parts of India, foreign cloth was burned in public demonstrations. Shops stopped selling British goods, and people began turning toward locally produced products.

The movement called on Indians to rely on their own industries, skills, and labor. Supporting Indian goods became both a political statement and a symbol of national pride.

Students, merchants, and ordinary citizens all joined the effort. Meetings and protests were organized in towns and cities, while newspapers and public speeches spread the message of economic self-reliance.

Writers, artists, and intellectuals also played a role in spreading nationalist feelings. The celebrated poet Rabindranath Tagore used songs, literature, and public gatherings to promote unity and pride in Indian culture.

What began as a protest against the partition of Bengal soon grew into something much larger. The Swadeshi movement helped turn Indian nationalism from an idea discussed by political leaders into a cause that ordinary people could take part in.

In the years that followed, the ideas behind Swadeshi, such as self-reliance, economic independence, and mass participation, continued to shape the growing struggle against British rule.

Later leaders such as Mahatma Gandhi would build on these ideas as the independence movement expanded across the country.

Chapter 6: Mahatma Gandhi

In many ways, India had been struggling against British rule since the very beginning of colonization, though an organized nationalist movement did not emerge until the late 19th century. It could be argued that the fight against colonial rule had been building for more than a century. But as we saw during the Sepoy Mutiny, overthrowing the British was not an easy task.

The Rebellion of 1857 represented widespread resistance to British authority, but it was not yet a unified nationalist movement seeking independence. Different groups had their own reasons for joining the uprising, and there was no single national leadership or shared political vision. Even so, the rebellion revealed how deep the resentment toward British rule had become. Although the British eventually suppressed the uprising, the desire for freedom did not disappear.

In the decades that followed, dissatisfaction with colonial rule continued to grow. Racism within the colonial system, economic hardships, and controversial British policies all added to the sense of frustration among Indians. Events like devastating famines and the partition of Bengal only deepened these grievances and helped fuel new calls for reform and self-government.

By the early 20th century, several developments had come together to strengthen the nationalist movement. An educated middle class had emerged, political organizations such as the Indian National Congress had been established, and new generations of Indians were becoming increasingly aware of their political rights.

What made this phase of the struggle different was the emergence of a group of educated leaders who could challenge the British on their own intellectual ground. Many of them were fluent in English, trained in Western political thought, and familiar with British law and institutions. They were ready to press their case for India's future.

Although many men and women contributed to India's independence, one figure would eventually become most closely associated with the movement.

Gandhi's Early Years and South Africa

Mahatma Gandhi, born Mohandas Karamchand Gandhi, was born in the coastal town of Porbandar in present-day Gujarat, India, on October 2nd, 1869. As a young boy, he loved reading Indian classics, and many of the stories centered around truth and moral courage left a deep impression on him. These early influences would shape the way he fought for India decades later.

A quiet and shy child, Gandhi was not known for being an outstanding student. He performed adequately in school and mostly kept to himself, often spending his time reading.

At the age of thirteen, he entered into an arranged marriage with Kasturbai Makhanji Kapadia, more commonly known as Kasturba Gandhi. The couple would go on to have four sons together: Harilal, Manilal, Ramdas, and Devdas.

After finishing school in Gujarat, Gandhi briefly attended Samaldas College in Bhavnagar. He soon left, however, and after encouragement from a family friend, he decided to pursue higher education in England. In 1888, he traveled to London to study law at the Inner Temple.

His decision to travel overseas angered members of his caste community, who believed crossing the sea would expose him to immoral Western influences. As a result, he was temporarily excommunicated.

Gandhi completed his legal studies, was called to the bar, and returned to India in 1891. His attempts to establish a law practice were not very successful, though. He struggled with confidence in the courtroom and often took on less important legal work to make a living.

In 1893, he accepted a job in South Africa, which was then under British rule. The assignment was supposed to last only a year, but Gandhi ended up spending much of the period between 1893 and 1914 there.

His time in South Africa proved to be a turning point in his life. Gandhi experienced prejudice and discrimination because of the color of his skin. For someone who had believed in the fairness of the British legal system and considered himself a loyal subject of the British Empire, these experiences were both shocking and eye-opening.

Gradually, he became deeply involved in the struggle for the rights of Indians living in South Africa. During these years, he began developing the philosophy that would later define his political approach, satyagraha, or nonviolent resistance.

In 1894, he helped establish the Natal Indian Congress, which allowed Indians in the region to organize politically and advocate for their rights. Although Europeans in South Africa were largely successful in limiting Indian voting rights, Gandhi's campaigns helped draw international attention to the treatment of Indians in the region.

Gandhi with the Natal Indian Congress, 1895.[16]

When Gandhi first arrived in South Africa, he had little interest in politics. However, his experiences there transformed him. By the time he returned to India in 1915, encouraged by his political mentor Gopal Krishna Gokhale, Gandhi was already respected as an activist who had successfully organized Indian communities abroad.

Gandhi in India

When Mahatma Gandhi returned to India and became active within the Indian National Congress, Britain was deeply embroiled in World War I. Gandhi's initial involvement in the Indian National Congress was largely observational, as he traveled across the country and familiarized himself with the issues and struggles facing ordinary Indians while also encouraging support for Britain's war effort.

Much like Gopal Krishna Gokhale, a Moderate leader of the Indian National Congress, Gandhi initially believed in a restrained and Moderate approach to reform. His education in England and familiarity with British legal traditions helped shape his belief that change could be pursued through moral pressure and lawful protest.

By 1920, Gandhi had become one of the most influential leaders within the Indian National Congress, and his strategy had shifted toward organized civil disobedience to press India's demands. This change in direction was strongly influenced by events that followed the passage of the Rowlatt Act in March 1919.

Under the Rowlatt Act, authorities were given sweeping powers to arrest and detain individuals suspected of political activism without trial. The law allowed the colonial government to imprison people without due process and placed severe restrictions on political activity. The act extended many of the emergency powers that had existed during the war under the Defence of India Act of 1915. However, instead of expiring after the war, these powers continued into peacetime and applied broadly to nationalist activism.

Indians who had strongly supported the British during the war were outraged by the decision. Their sense of betrayal only deepened in the months that followed, particularly after the tragic events of the Jallianwala Bagh massacre, also known as the Amritsar massacre.

Jallianwala Bagh Massacre

The massacre took place on April 13th, 1919, at Jallianwala Bagh in the city of Amritsar. A large crowd had gathered there, many of them celebrating the Baisakhi festival, alongside others who had come to protest against the Rowlatt Act.

Brigadier General Reginald Dyer marched into the enclosed garden with troops from the British Indian Army. Without issuing a warning, he ordered his soldiers to fire into the crowd.

Chaos followed. People tried to flee, but the narrow exits made escape difficult. The troops continued firing for several minutes. Official British reports stated that 379 people were killed and more than 1,200 were injured, though Indian estimates placed the number of dead much higher, possibly over a thousand.

The brutality of the massacre shocked the country. Many Indians were horrified not only by the violence itself but also by the lack of remorse shown by the authorities afterward.

The event caused outrage even in Britain. Winston Churchill, who was serving as secretary of state for war, condemned the massacre in Parliament. A government investigation known as the Hunter Commission was later established to examine Dyer's actions. Although the inquiry criticized Dyer, the punishment he received was limited, and many Indians felt justice had not been served.

The massacre dramatically intensified opposition to British rule. Anger spread across the country, and many Indians began looking for a new way to challenge colonial authority.

It was in this atmosphere that Mahatma Gandhi emerged as a national leader. Gandhi called for satyagraha, a form of nonviolent political resistance based on the belief that moral courage and collective refusal to cooperate with injustice could be more powerful than force.

Gandhi's philosophy rested on a few simple but powerful principles. Injustice must be resisted, but never through violence. Suffering endured with dignity could awaken the conscience of the oppressor. And ordinary people acting together could force even the most powerful empire to listen.

At the time, these ideas seemed radical. Yet they would soon transform India's struggle for independence.

Non-Cooperation Movement

Organized by Mahatma Gandhi with the support of the Indian National Congress, the Non-Cooperation Movement began in 1920 as a mass protest against British rule.

The movement expanded on earlier ideas of boycott and self-reliance that had appeared during the Swadeshi movement. People were urged to boycott British goods and to refuse to participate in colonial institutions. Students left government schools, lawyers refused to practice in British courts, and many government employees resigned from their posts.

After decades of frustration with colonial rule, many Indians finally felt they had a way to express their opposition. The movement spread rapidly, and large numbers of people across the country began participating in protests, boycotts, and acts of nonviolent resistance. For the first time, the nationalist struggle was no longer limited mainly to educated elites. The Non-Cooperation Movement transformed it into a nationwide mass movement involving peasants, workers, merchants, and students. The movement also established Gandhi as the central figure of India's independence struggle and the most influential leader within the Indian National Congress.

The campaign came to an abrupt end in 1922 following the Chauri Chaura incident. What had begun as a peaceful protest escalated into violence when demonstrators clashed with police and burned a police station, killing several officers. Deeply disturbed by the violence, Gandhi immediately called off the movement.

Later that year, Gandhi was arrested on charges of sedition and sentenced to six years in prison. He ultimately served about two years before being released in 1924. Upon his release, Gandhi briefly served as president of the Indian National Congress.

By this time, the political landscape of India had begun to change. Cooperation between Hindu and Muslim political groups had weakened, and the Indian National Congress itself continued to debate the best strategy for achieving independence.

Purna Swaraj

Following more than a decade of protests, political movements, and continued frustrations with British rule, many leaders within the Indian National Congress felt that the time for Moderate demands had passed. Tensions had grown steadily during the 1920s, particularly after the arrival of the Simon Commission in 1928, a British body sent to discuss constitutional reform in India but one that contained no Indian members. Its exclusion of Indians provoked widespread outrage and protests across the country.

During one such demonstration in Lahore, police attempted to disperse the crowd with a brutal lathi charge, beating protesters with heavy wooden batons. Among those injured was the respected nationalist leader Lala Lajpat Rai, who had been leading the protest. He suffered serious injuries during the assault and died several weeks later. Many Indians believed his death had been caused by the police attack, and the incident further intensified anger toward British rule.

The lack of meaningful reforms and the continued suppression of political rights had inflamed public opinion. Within the Indian National Congress, there was growing agreement that India must demand complete independence rather than limited reforms under British authority.

In 1929, Jawaharlal Nehru was elected president of the Indian National Congress. Under his leadership, the party formally adopted the goal of full independence from Britain.

As a symbol of this new direction, on New Year's Eve in 1929, Nehru hoisted the Indian flag in Lahore on the banks of the Ravi River, a city that is now part of modern-day Pakistan. Congress leaders then read out a pledge of independence to the gathered crowd. The pledge declared that Indians had the right to freedom and the right to enjoy the fruits of their own labor and the resources of their country. It called for justice, self-rule, and an end to British authority in India.

Nehru in Lahore addressing the crowd.[16]

Although the pledge was not a legal declaration of independence, it was still a powerful political statement. When the crowd was asked if they supported the resolution, the response was overwhelming.

To mark this commitment, the Indian National Congress declared that January 26th, 1930, would be celebrated across India as Independence Day. Across the country, people began raising the Indian flag and pledging their support for complete independence. Nationalist sentiment surged, and many Indians believed a new chapter in their country's history was about to begin.

On January 26th, 1930, the Indian National Congress formally passed what became known as the Purna Swaraj resolution. The phrase, derived from Sanskrit, means complete self-rule or total independence. By passing it, the Indian National Congress made its position unmistakably clear. They were no longer asking for reforms within the British system or for greater representation at the table. They wanted the British gone and India returned to its people.

Despite the declaration, the British government refused to recognize India's claim to independence. In response, Mahatma Gandhi began preparing a new campaign of civil disobedience. With the support of other leaders in the independence movement, he planned to mobilize the population through nonviolent protest.

Gandhi chose an unlikely issue to rally the nation: salt. Although some members of the Indian National Congress were initially skeptical, his plan to challenge the British salt monopoly would soon lead to one of the most famous acts of protest in modern history.

Salt and India

To understand why the Salt March became such a powerful moment in India's struggle for independence, it helps to look back at the long history of salt in India and its complicated relationship with taxation.

Salt had been taxed in India long before the arrival of the British. During the Mughal Empire, for example, duties were collected on salt in several regions, including Bengal. Both Hindus and Muslims were required to pay the tax.

Salt itself was plentiful across the Indian subcontinent. For centuries, it had been produced naturally in many areas. The coastal regions of Odisha and the vast salt flats of the Rann of Kutch were well known for producing large quantities of high-quality salt.

When the East India Company began expanding its control over India, salt quickly became an important source of revenue. After the Battle of Plassey and later the Battle of Buxar, the EIC gained control over major revenue systems in Bengal and surrounding regions. Recognizing the profit that could be made, EIC officials began placing taxes and rents on salt production and trade. At one point, Robert Clive granted monopolies over commodities like salt and tobacco to high-ranking East India Company officials.

The system soon became notorious for corruption and was later replaced by tighter government control over the salt trade. Under this system, salt had to be brought to designated government depots where merchants and traders could purchase it. The monopoly generated enormous profits for the colonial administration but disrupted the livelihoods of local producers and traders who had previously controlled the salt trade.

The people who suffered most were the poor. Salt was an everyday necessity, yet the taxes made it increasingly expensive for ordinary families.

Not surprisingly, smuggling soon became common. To enforce the salt tax, the British created an extensive customs barrier that stretched across northern India. Known as the Great Hedge of India, it was made of dense thorn bushes and trees and guarded by thousands of customs officers who patrolled the line to prevent illegal salt trade.

Even after the East India Company lost control of India following the Indian Rebellion of 1857, the British government continued the salt monopoly and kept the tax firmly in place. The system was further reinforced by the Indian Salt Act 1882, which gave the colonial government strict control over the production and sale of salt. Producing or selling salt without authorization became illegal, and offenders could face fines or imprisonment.

By the early 20th century, India was producing well over a million tons of salt each year, yet Indians were still forced to buy it through the government monopoly and pay the tax imposed by the colonial authorities.

Salt was a basic necessity of life, something produced naturally from the land and sea. Yet Indians were forbidden from collecting or producing it. To many, the salt laws became a clear example of how unjust and intrusive British rule had become.

Salt Satyagraha

When Mahatma Gandhi proposed the Salt March (Salt Satyagraha), he chose a cause that was close to the hearts of ordinary Indians and easy to unite around. For centuries, salt had been taxed in India in one form or another. To many Indians, the idea of rising up against that system and defeating it must have felt like an impossible dream, nearly as impossible as achieving independence itself. Perhaps symbolically, Gandhi believed that the ability to use something as simple as salt without restriction would represent a kind of freedom.

Whatever his personal reasoning for choosing salt as the focus of civil disobedience, the decision proved remarkably effective. Salt was something every Indian needed. It did not divide people along religious or caste lines, and it affected the poor the most—the very people Gandhi hoped to mobilize. And what Gandhi needed more than anything was large numbers of ordinary people willing to quietly resist.

About a month before the march, newspapers began reporting Gandhi's plan. It was straightforward but bold. He intended to lead a twenty-four-day march to the coastal village of Dandi in Gujarat, on the Arabian Sea. There, on April 6th, he would deliberately break the salt laws.

The date was not chosen at random. April 6th held meaning for Gandhi because it marked the anniversary of the nationwide strike that had taken place in 1919 to protest the Rowlatt Act. Gandhi encouraged people to join the march and regularly spoke with newspapers and journalists, ensuring that word of the plan spread widely.

The route was carefully planned. Gandhi and his companions would travel through dozens of villages across several districts. Supporters went ahead of the march to arrange places for rest stops and public gatherings where Gandhi could address the crowds. As the preparations unfolded, newspapers across India followed the story closely, and international journalists began to take notice.

A few days before the march began, Gandhi made one final appeal to the viceroy of India, Edward Wood, 1st Earl of Halifax. In a letter, he laid out a list of demands, including the reduction of the salt tax. He suggested that if the government addressed these grievances, the march might not be necessary. Lord Irwin declined to accept the demands, and no meeting took place.

On March 12th, 1930, Gandhi began what he called his salt satyagraha. He set out from his ashram (a communal settlement devoted to simple living) with seventy-eight carefully chosen followers. These men had been selected for their discipline and commitment to nonviolence.

Dressed in simple white homespun clothes, Gandhi and his companions made a striking sight as they walked from village to village. Observers often described the group as looking like a slow-moving white stream flowing through the countryside.

The march covered roughly 400 kilometers (250 miles) and remained peaceful throughout. As the days passed, newspapers printed photographs and reports of Gandhi's progress, drawing increasing attention from readers around the world. At each stop, he was welcomed by large crowds. He slept in the open, ate simple meals, and spoke to villagers about freedom, self-reliance, and the power of nonviolent resistance.

Gandhi and his followers during the Salt March of 1930.[17]

More and more people began joining the procession. What had started as a small group slowly grew into a much larger demonstration, with supporters gathering in towns and villages to show their support. By the time Gandhi reached Dandi on April 5th, 1930, the march had captured the country's imagination.

The next morning, April 6th, Gandhi walked to the shore of the Arabian Sea. In a quiet but deliberate act of defiance, he bent down and picked up a small lump of natural salt that had formed along the coast, publicly breaking the British salt laws. To drive the point home, he later boiled seawater to produce salt himself, encouraging others across the country to do the same.

Journalists quickly sent reports of the event around the world. With that simple gesture, Gandhi had ignited a movement. Across India, millions of people began defying the salt laws by producing their own salt or buying it illegally.

With a single handful of salt, Gandhi had challenged the authority of the British Empire and inspired a wave of civil disobedience that spread across the country.

Civil Disobedience

After the Salt March, Gandhi turned his attention to organizing the next phase of the movement. He set up a makeshift base near Dandi and began planning further acts of civil disobedience, including a planned protest at the government-controlled salt works in Dharasana.

However, before Gandhi and his followers could reach Dharasana, he, along with thousands of other activists and leaders, was arrested by the British authorities.

Gandhi's arrest sparked outrage across the country. Protests broke out nationwide, and the planned march to the Dharasana Salt Works went ahead as planned under other leaders. The British response, particularly the violent treatment of unarmed protesters, drew sharp criticism from around the world.

The Salt Satyagraha quickly spread beyond the original march and evolved into a nationwide campaign of civil disobedience. In some cities, including Karachi and Calcutta, protests occasionally escalated into violent clashes that resulted in deaths and injuries. Gandhi repeatedly urged restraint and insisted that the movement remain nonviolent, but the campaign of civil disobedience continued to grow as more and more Indians joined the struggle.

Women also played an important role in the movement. Many became activists, picketers, and protestors, while others took part in producing illegal salt. With Gandhi's encouragement, women in Bombay organized pickets outside shops that sold foreign cloth and liquor.

With millions of people defying colonial laws and demonstrations spreading across the country, British authorities struggled to contain a movement that had grown far larger than they had anticipated.

Irwin-Gandhi Pact

The British understood that the situation could not continue indefinitely. The movement had spread across the country, and the colonial government was struggling to contain it. Viceroy Edward Wood was eager to find a way to bring the unrest to an end. The attempt to crush the movement through arrests and repression had not succeeded, and it had become increasingly clear that some form of negotiation would be necessary.

In London, the government under Prime Minister Ramsay MacDonald recognized that meaningful discussions about India's future could not take place without the involvement of Gandhi and the Indian National Congress. Lord Irwin, therefore, authorized the unconditional release of Gandhi and many other Congress leaders who had been imprisoned during the civil disobedience campaign.

Following his release, Gandhi agreed to meet with the viceroy, and the Indian National Congress authorized him to negotiate on its behalf. A series of discussions took place over several weeks as both sides attempted to find common ground.

An agreement was eventually reached, and on March 5th, 1931, the Gandhi–Irwin Pact was formally signed.

India did not gain the independence many had hoped for, but the agreement did include several important concessions. Political prisoners who had been jailed for acts of nonviolent protest were to be released, and the restrictions placed on the Indian National Congress and its activities were lifted.

On the issue of salt, the pact allowed Indians living along the coast to collect or produce small quantities of salt for their own use. This was a limited but still symbolically important concession. The British government also agreed to allow peaceful political activity, including picketing, to resume.

In return, Gandhi agreed to suspend the civil disobedience movement and to attend the upcoming constitutional discussions in London. These discussions were part of the Second Round Table Conference, one of a series of meetings organized by the British government to debate possible constitutional reforms for India.

Although the pact did not deliver the complete independence that many Indians desired (what the Indian National Congress had called Purna Swaraj), it was still seen by many as an important step forward. For the first time, representatives of the Indian nationalist movement would participate directly in discussions about the country's political future.

Just as importantly, the events surrounding the Salt March had shown that organized, nonviolent resistance could force the British government to negotiate. For many Indians, that realization alone strengthened their belief that independence was no longer an impossible dream.

Gandhi's Later Years

Unfortunately, participation in the Second Round Table Conference did not go as well as many in the Indian National Congress had hoped. During the discussions in London, Gandhi pressed for Britain to recognize India's right to full independence. However, the British government was not prepared to make such a concession.

After Gandhi returned to India, the brief period of relative calm soon came to an end. Political tensions quickly resurfaced, and under the new viceroy, Freeman Freeman-Thomas, 1ˢᵗ Marquess of Willingdon, the colonial government once again took a harsher approach. Repressive measures were again introduced, and the civil disobedience movement resumed.

Soon afterward, Gandhi was arrested. The cycle of protest and repression continued for several years. By 1934, the civil disobedience movement began to lose momentum after years of arrests, government crackdowns, and growing fatigue. Eventually, it came to an end.

Even after the civil disobedience movement faded, Gandhi remained a central figure in the struggle for independence. In 1942, he launched the Quit India Movement, calling on the British to leave India immediately and return control of the country to its people. The movement sparked protests and unrest across India and was met with swift and severe repression. Tens of thousands of people were arrested, including Gandhi and many other leaders of the Indian National Congress. Many lives were lost during the crackdown. Yet even in the face of that repression, the movement made it clear that the question was no longer whether India would become free, but when.

As independence drew closer, Gandhi faced one of the most painful challenges of his life. Relations between Hindus and Muslims had deteriorated sharply, and the possibility of partition—the division of British India into separate nations—loomed large. Gandhi was deeply opposed to the idea. In the final years before independence, he traveled tirelessly through some of the most violence-stricken regions of the country, pleading with communities to put aside their hatred and live together as neighbors.

It was a battle he ultimately could not win. In 1947, British India was divided into two new nations: India and Pakistan. The violence and displacement that accompanied this partition left Gandhi heartbroken.

Assassination of Gandhi

On January 30th, 1948, at the age of seventy-eight, Mahatma Gandhi's long struggle for India came to an abrupt end when he was assassinated while walking to an interfaith prayer meeting.

Gandhi was in the habit of holding daily prayer gatherings at Birla House in New Delhi. On that evening, he was walking toward the prayer platform when a man stepped out from the waiting crowd and fired a pistol at him at close range. Three shots were fired. Gandhi was struck in the chest and abdomen and collapsed. He was carried back into the house, but the wounds were fatal, and he died almost immediately.

Gandhi was no stranger to assassination attempts. Several earlier plots against his life had failed over the years. Sadly, this time, the attempt succeeded.

The assassin was quickly seized by members of the crowd. The man was Nathuram Godse, a Hindu nationalist who strongly opposed Gandhi's efforts to promote cooperation and peace between India's religious communities, particularly between Hindus and Muslims. Godse had been influenced by radical nationalist ideas that argued India should be a Hindu nation and that Gandhi's policies toward Muslims had weakened the country.

He and several accomplices were arrested, put on trial, and ultimately convicted. Some of the accused later appealed their convictions; two men were acquitted. Godse himself appealed the sentence, but the verdict was upheld. He and one of his co-conspirators were executed on November 15th, 1949.

Gandhi's sudden and violent death shocked the world. Tributes poured in from across the globe. Jawaharlal Nehru addressed the nation in a radio broadcast announcing the tragedy.

More than two million people joined Gandhi's funeral procession as it moved through the streets of Delhi, and millions more around the world mourned the loss of the man who had become the moral voice of India's struggle for freedom.

Gandhi's Legacy

Gandhi's influence and the legacy he left behind continue to be felt to this day. Often referred to in India as the "Father of the Nation," he is widely remembered as the man who helped give birth to modern India.

His political activism and his principles of nonviolent protest were instrumental in transforming the struggle for independence into a mass movement. Gandhi's campaigns of civil disobedience showed millions of ordinary people that resistance could take many forms and that unity and moral courage could challenge even the most powerful empire.

Mahatma Gandhi in 1931.[18]

His ideas traveled far beyond India. Leaders such as Martin Luther King Jr. in the United States and Nelson Mandela in South Africa drew inspiration from Gandhi's philosophy of nonviolent resistance in their own struggles for justice and equality.

Gandhi faced violence and oppression with quiet determination. He believed that real strength could come not from weapons or armies but from the collective will of ordinary people acting together.

At the same time, Gandhi was not without controversy. Historians continue to debate aspects of his views and actions, including his early writings in South Africa, his complicated stance on the caste system, and some of his personal choices later in life. Like many figures who shaped history, his legacy is both influential and complex.

Yet despite those debates, Gandhi's impact on the 20th century remains undeniable. He showed that a single voice, guided by conviction and moral courage, could inspire millions and alter the course of history.

That is the legacy he left behind.

Chapter 7: World War I and the Interwar Years

On June 28th, 1914, the assassination of Archduke Franz Ferdinand of Austria-Hungary set off a chain of events that would soon reshape the entire world. What began as a political crisis in Europe quickly grew into something much larger, and its effects would eventually impact India.

After the assassination, Austria-Hungary declared war on Serbia. Within days, other powers were pulled into the conflict. Germany declared war on Russia and France. German forces marched through neutral Belgium to invade France.

The invasion of Belgium forced Britain to act. On August 4th, 1914, Britain declared war on Germany. Because India was part of the British Empire, it, too, was drawn into the war.

Indian soldiers were mobilized quickly. Within weeks, they were being sent overseas to fight for the empire. Many would soon find themselves on the battlefields of Europe, far from home.

What had started as a regional conflict soon spiraled into a global war that would last for more than four years. From the beginning of the war in 1914 to its end in 1918, India played a major role in supporting Britain and its allies. Indian soldiers fought in Europe, the Middle East, and Africa. The country also supplied money, food, and materials for the war effort. Field Marshal Sir Claude Auchinleck later remarked that Britain could not have fought the world wars without the support of the Indian Army.

British Indian Army and WWI

Before the First World War, the British Indian Army had roughly 240,000 men, including regular soldiers and reserves. This made it one of the largest volunteer armies in the world. Most of the time, the army was used to maintain order within India or to guard the empire's frontier, especially along the border with Afghanistan.

When war broke out in Europe in 1914, India quickly became part of the British war effort. In total, about 1.3 million Indian soldiers and laborers were mobilized and sent overseas to serve alongside British forces.

Indian troops arrived in Europe as early as 1914, at a time when Britain was desperately short of manpower. They soon found themselves fighting in some of the war's hardest battles, including Ypres and Neuve Chapelle. Later in the war, Indian cavalry units also took part in the fighting around the Somme.

Indian soldiers did not fight only in Europe. They were also sent to other parts of the empire, including Egypt and German East Africa. The largest campaign took place in Mesopotamia, where roughly 700,000 Indian troops served in the long struggle against the Ottoman Empire. By taking over much of the fighting in these distant regions, Indian forces helped free British troops for the main battles in Europe.

Indian bicycle troops at a crossroads on the Fricourt-Mametz Road, Somme, France, July 1916.[19]

The cost of the war was high. Around seventy-four thousand Indian soldiers lost their lives, and many more were wounded or listed as missing.

Even after the war ended in Europe in 1918, the Indian Army was still being used in military campaigns. In 1919, Indian troops fought in the Third Afghan War, and they continued to serve in a series of frontier conflicts through the 1920s and 1930s.

During the First World War, eleven Victoria Crosses were awarded to Indian soldiers for acts of exceptional bravery. This recognition carried special meaning. Before 1911, Indian soldiers were not eligible for the Victoria Cross, which had largely been reserved for European troops.

Not all of India's contributions came from soldiers on the battlefield, though. Hundreds of thousands of laborers also supported the war effort. They dug trenches, built roads and railways, carried supplies, worked in medical camps, and produced clothing and equipment for the troops.

India also supplied the empire with vast quantities of raw materials. Cotton, leather, jute, and tea were shipped to Britain for military use or to sell to support the war economy. In addition, India contributed about 146 million pounds to Britain's war effort, which helped finance the struggle.

These demands placed a heavy strain on India's economy and deepened the hardships many people were already facing. Yet many Indian leaders and communities supported the war effort, hoping that loyalty to Britain would lead to greater political rights once the fighting was over.

Defence of India Act 1915

While the war raged in Europe, life in India was becoming increasingly tense. The country was already struggling with questions about its future and its place in the British Empire. As the war dragged on, more Indians began to wonder why they were still expected to live under British rule.

Many Indians were fighting and dying for Britain in the war. In return, they hoped to gain greater respect and equality within the empire. Instead, British officials tightened their control over the country. In 1915, the government passed the Defence of India Act. It was introduced as a temporary wartime measure meant to suppress revolutionary activity and possible German-backed plots in India.

However, the law also gave the colonial government sweeping powers. Authorities could arrest people suspected of revolutionary ties and hold them without trial. Special tribunals were created, and normal legal protections were weakened. The government expanded surveillance across the country. Public meetings, political gatherings, and newspaper publications were closely monitored and restricted.

Many Indians were upset at these policies. The heavy economic burden of the war and the rising number of casualties only deepened the growing resentment toward British rule.

When the Defence of India Act was about to expire after the war, the British government introduced another law. In 1919, they passed the Rowlatt Act. This new law extended many of the same emergency powers that had existed during the war and was designed to suppress revolutionary and nationalist movements.

The law sparked outrage across India. Protests erupted in many cities. The anger it created would soon contribute to one of the most shocking events of the colonial period, the Amritsar or Jallianwala Bagh massacre of 1919. The crisis also pushed Mahatma Gandhi to begin organizing a nationwide campaign of nonviolent resistance against British rule.

Lucknow Pact of 1916

Although Muslims and Hindus had lived side by side in India for centuries, their relationship was not always easy. At times, they cooperated and shared communities, but there were also tensions and disagreements. Under British rule, these differences often grew more pronounced, as colonial policies sometimes deepened the divide between the two communities.

One important turning point came with the partition of Bengal in 1905. The British divided the province into two parts, creating a new province of East Bengal, where Muslims formed the majority. Many Muslims supported the change because it promised them greater political influence. However, many Hindus strongly opposed it, and the decision sparked widespread protests.

The political tension of this period encouraged Muslim leaders to organize more formally. In 1906, they founded the All-India Muslim League to represent Muslim political interests.

At the same time, the Indian National Congress was dealing with its own internal issues. In 1907, the party split into two factions after disagreements over strategy and leadership. Some Congress leaders soon realized that if they wanted to challenge British rule, they first needed to restore unity within their own ranks.

The Muslim League had initially been fairly loyal to the British government. But over time, many Muslim leaders grew disappointed with British policies. The British decision to reverse the partition of Bengal in 1911 due to the political backlash angered many Muslims who had supported it. During World War I, Britain's war against the Ottoman Empire troubled many Muslims since the Ottoman sultan was widely seen as the leader of the Islamic world.

Slowly, leaders in both communities began to see the value of cooperation. They believed that if Indians hoped to win greater political rights, they would have to present a united front.

This cooperation reached an important moment in December 1916. At a meeting in Lucknow, leaders of the Indian National Congress and the All-India Muslim League agreed to work together. The agreement became known as the Lucknow Pact.

Bal Gangadhar Tilak represented the Indian National Congress during the negotiations, while Muhammad Ali Jinnah played a key role for the All-India Muslim League. At the time, Jinnah was widely praised as the "Ambassador of Hindu-Muslim Unity," a title that reflected how hopeful many people felt about the agreement.

The Lucknow Pact laid out a plan for greater Indian participation in government. It called for expanded legislative councils and greater representation for Indians. It also guaranteed that Muslims would receive one-third of the seats in the central legislature, ensuring their political voice would be protected.

The agreement was not perfect, but it helped ease tensions between Congress factions and encouraged cooperation between the Indian National Congress and the All-India Muslim League. For a time, it gave Indian leaders a stronger and more united position from which to press the British government for reform.

Indian Home Rule Movement

Before Gandhi emerged as the dominant voice of the independence movement, leaders within the Indian National Congress had already spent years pushing for greater self-government. One important effort was the Indian Home Rule movement, led by Bal Gangadhar Tilak and Annie Besant, a British socialist, reformer, and activist.

Besant first came to India through her work with the Theosophical Society, an organization that sought to foster peace. While living there, she became aware of the inequality between the British rulers and the Indian population. Over time, she began to speak openly in favor of Indian self-government and eventually joined the growing nationalist movement.

The First World War created new tensions inside India. Some leaders believed that supporting Britain in the war might lead to political reforms afterward. Others believed the war showed just how unfair the relationship between Britain and India had become. Indians were being asked to fight and sacrifice for the empire while still being denied meaningful political power.

Tilak and Besant argued that the time had come for India to demand self-rule. They began pressing the British government for a clear path toward greater political authority for Indians. However, with the war raging in Europe, Britain showed little interest in making major changes.

In response, the Home Rule movement began to take shape.

A crowd waiting for Tilak in Madras.[30]

The movement was inspired in part by Irish Home Rule. Its main goal was to achieve self-government for India within the British Empire. To achieve this, leaders focused on educating the public, organizing meetings, and encouraging ordinary Indians to become involved in politics.

Tilak and Besant formed Home Rule Leagues across the country. Through speeches, pamphlets, and public gatherings, they spread the idea that Indians had the right to govern themselves. The movement gained strong momentum between 1916 and 1918, helping to revive nationalist enthusiasm across India.

In 1917, the British government placed Annie Besant under arrest for her role in leading the Home Rule movement. The decision caused widespread outrage and protests across the country. The backlash forced British officials to pay closer attention to the growing political unrest in India.

That same year, Edwin Montagu, the newly appointed secretary of state for India, made an important announcement in the British Parliament. He declared that Britain would work toward the gradual development of self-governing institutions in India and allow Indians a greater role in government. This statement later became the foundation for the Government of India Act passed in 1919.

Although the Home Rule movement played an important role in reviving Indian nationalism, it gradually faded as a new leader began to rise within the Indian National Congress. When Gandhi became more actively involved in the struggle, his campaigns of mass protest and civil disobedience quickly captured the nation's attention.

Even so, the Home Rule movement had left its mark. It helped rebuild unity within the Indian National Congress, encouraged cooperation between political factions, and brought new energy into the nationalist cause. By the time Gandhi stepped onto the national stage, the idea of self-government had spread widely across India, and the country was ready for the next phase of the struggle for independence.

Government of India Acts 1919 and 1935

Partly in response to growing pressure from nationalist movements such as the Home Rule campaign, the British Parliament passed the Government of India Act in 1919. The reforms are often called the Montagu-Chelmsford Reforms, named after Edwin Montagu, Secretary of State for India, and Lord Chelmsford, Viceroy of India, who worked together on the plan.

The act promised that Britain would slowly introduce responsible government in India and allow Indians to take a larger role in politics. It also committed to reviewing the reforms after ten years.

Under the new system, legislative councils at both the central and provincial levels were expanded and given greater authority. The act also introduced a system known as diarchy, or shared rule, in the provinces. Some areas of government were placed under Indian ministers, while others remained under British control.

The act also called for the creation of a Public Service Commission to oversee the hiring and management of civil servants. This commission was eventually established in 1926.

British officials believed the reforms were a major step forward and were not eager to make further changes. Many Indian leaders disagreed. The Indian National Congress and other political groups argued that the act did not go far enough. They believed it left real power in British hands. Their demand for self-rule remained unchanged.

As the years passed, pressure on the British government continued to grow across India. Nationalist movements expanded, and Gandhi's campaigns of civil disobedience brought millions of Indians into politics. Faced with this growing unrest, Britain introduced a new round of reforms with the Government of India Act of 1935.

The 1935 act introduced far more sweeping changes than the earlier reforms. In fact, it was the longest act ever passed by the British Parliament at the time, containing 321 sections and 10 schedules. Many of the ideas in the act were later used when India created its own government after independence.

One of the most important changes was the end of the diarchy in the provinces. Provincial governments were given greater authority, and elected Indian leaders were able to take a larger role in running them. However, British governors still held significant power and could step in if they believed imperial interests were at risk.

The act also reorganized parts of the empire. Burma was separated from India, and two new provinces, Sindh and Orissa, were created from existing territories.

The Federal Court was established, and plans were introduced for an All-India Federation that would bring together British-ruled provinces and the princely states under one central government. However, many of the princes were not willing to join the arrangement, and the federation never came into effect.

Provincial elections were held in 1937 under the new system. The Indian National Congress won major victories and formed governments in several provinces. The results showed how much support the independence movement had gained across the country.

Even with these reforms, the most important powers, such as defense, foreign policy, and major financial decisions, still remained in British hands. For many Indians, this was no longer enough. They wanted full authority over their own country. And as the days passed, they increasingly wanted the British to leave altogether.

The League of Nations and India

Another development that strengthened India's desire for independence was its role in the League of Nations.

After the First World War ended with the signing of the Treaty of Versailles, the destruction was enormous, and the world did not want to see anything like it again. The major Allied powers believed countries needed a way to work together and prevent another global war.

At the Paris Peace Conference, world leaders worked to create a new international organization that could help resolve disputes between nations. The idea was strongly supported by US President Woodrow Wilson, and the League of Nations was officially established in 1920.

The League of Nations began with more than forty member states. Among them were Brazil, Canada, and New Zealand. India was also included as a founding member, even though it was still under British rule.

The situation made little sense. India was allowed to sit among independent nations and take part in international discussions, but its representatives were still chosen and directed by the British government.

Indian nationalists were quick to notice the irony. India was being presented to the world as a participant in global affairs, yet it still had no control over its own government at home. For many, this only strengthened their determination to gain full independence. The contradiction was impossible to ignore.

At the same time, taking part in the League of Nations gave India its first real taste of international diplomacy. Indian delegates joined committees, attended meetings, and began building connections with representatives from other countries.

These early experiences proved useful later on. When India eventually gained independence, its leaders already had some experience dealing with other nations and navigating the world of international politics.

Chapter 8: World War II and the Quit India Movement

The end of the First World War did not end military campaigns for India's British Army. Britain continued to use its colonial forces in different operations across the empire, especially along India's northwestern frontier, well into the 1930s.

At the same time, many nations were trying to avoid another major war. The devastation of the First World War was still fresh in people's minds. European powers hoped that diplomacy and compromise could preserve peace.

This thinking shaped how Britain and France responded to Adolf Hitler's early actions. Both countries followed a policy that later became known as appeasement. They avoided direct confrontation even as Hitler openly violated the terms of the Treaty of Versailles. Hitler first annexed Austria in 1938. Soon after, Germany occupied Czechoslovakia. Britain and France protested, but they did not take military action.

The situation changed when Germany invaded Poland on September 1ˢᵗ, 1939. This time, Britain and France could not ignore Hitler's aggression. They issued ultimatums demanding that Germany withdraw its forces. When Germany refused, both countries declared war on September 3ʳᵈ, 1939. The world was once again at war.

As soon as Britain declared war, Lord Linlithgow, India's viceroy from 1936 to 1943, announced that India would also be joining the war effort.

The decision was made without consulting Indian political leaders. Many in India were angered that the country had been dragged into another imperial war without its consent.

The Indian National Congress reacted strongly. In protest, Congress ministries governing seven provinces resigned between October and November 1939. Their resignations weakened the British government's authority in India.

Congress leaders argued that Linlithgow's proclamation made a mockery of the reforms promised under

Lord Linlithgow.[21]

the Government of India Acts. The British had claimed that India was slowly moving toward self-rule, yet when war came, Indian leaders were not even consulted.

The Indian National Congress made it clear that it was willing to support Britain's war effort, but it demanded something in return. If India was expected to fight in the war, Britain would first have to promise independence.

The 1940 August Offer

Britain could not, or rather would not, promise India full independence. Instead, it tried to find a middle ground. In August 1940, Lord Linlithgow announced what became known as the August Offer.

The proposal promised to expand the viceroy's Executive Council to include more Indians. It also suggested the creation of a war council that would serve in an advisory role. Most importantly, it said that after the war, Indians would have the right to frame and draft their own constitution.

To British officials, this seemed like a reasonable compromise. To leaders in the Indian National Congress, it sounded like little more than empty words. Some members of Congress wanted to respond by launching another civil disobedience movement. Gandhi hesitated. He feared that a mass movement during wartime could quickly turn violent.

Instead, Gandhi proposed something different. He called it Individual Satyagraha. Rather than launching a mass movement, individuals would publicly speak out against the war and assert their right to free speech. The protest would remain peaceful and limited in scope.

Gandhi carefully chose the first satyagrahis, selecting men he trusted to remain disciplined and committed to nonviolence. The first was Vinoba Bhave, a devoted follower known for his calm and spiritual character. Soon after, Jawaharlal Nehru also spoke out.

British authorities responded quickly. The satyagrahis were arrested for violating wartime restrictions under the Defence of India Act of 1939 and sent to prison.

The arrests did not stop the movement. Others stepped forward to take their place. By mid-1941, roughly twenty thousand to twenty-five thousand people had been arrested for taking part in the protests.

Cripps Mission of 1942

When it became clear that the August Offer had failed to win India's support, Britain faced a new problem in the war. Japan had now entered the conflict and was advancing quickly across Asia. British leaders feared that India might soon be threatened as well. Securing India's support suddenly became far more urgent.

In 1942, the British government sent Sir Stafford Cripps to India to negotiate with the Indian National Congress and the All-India Muslim League. His mission soon became known as the Cripps Mission.

Cripps brought a new proposal. Britain promised that after the war, India would receive full dominion status. This meant India would govern itself while remaining part of the British Commonwealth. Indians would also be allowed to write their own constitution.

However, the plan included an important condition. Provinces would have the right to opt out of the new Indian union if they wished. This suggested that Britain might accept the creation of a separate Muslim state in the future.

By now, trust between Indian leaders and the British government was very weak. The Indian National Congress rejected the proposal. Its leaders opposed delaying independence until after the war. They also strongly objected to allowing provinces to break away from a future Indian union.

The All-India Muslim League also rejected the offer. The proposal allowed provinces to opt out, but it did not clearly promise the creation of a Muslim state. League leaders believed the plan did not go far enough to protect Muslim interests.

The negotiations quickly broke down, and the Cripps Mission ended in failure. Frustration and anger across India continued to grow.

Quit India Movement of 1942

When negotiations between Britain and Indian leaders broke down, the Indian National Congress began to believe that talks would lead nowhere. Gandhi and other leaders concluded that the only way forward was to launch a mass movement against British rule. Britain was deeply tied up in the war, and Japan was advancing across Asia. Many in Congress believed the British position in India had weakened. They felt the moment had come for a final push toward freedom.

On August 8th, 1942, the All India Congress Committee met in Bombay. During the meeting, Gandhi's Quit India resolution was passed. In his speech that day, Gandhi urged Indians to free the country or die trying. His message became famous as the call to "Do or Die."

Not everyone in Congress was fully comfortable with the decision. Some leaders, including Jawaharlal Nehru, had worries about launching such a movement during wartime. However, once the resolution passed, they stood behind Gandhi and supported the effort.

Outside the Indian National Congress, support was limited. The All-India Muslim League refused to back the movement. Muhammad Ali Jinnah instead reaffirmed the Muslim League's support for Britain and the war effort. Many of the princely states also stayed loyal to the British.

Despite this lack of support, the Indian National Congress moved forward. The resolution's demand was clear and direct. Britain must leave India immediately. India would no longer accept imperial rule and intended to become a sovereign nation. The challenge was especially bold because it came during the middle of the Second World War.

Gandhi's words spread quickly across the country. His call for freedom stirred millions. Protests soon broke out in many parts of India. Some demonstrations remained peaceful, but others turned violent. Crowds attacked police stations, damaged rail lines and railway stations, and targeted government buildings. Many people also boycotted British institutions and activities connected to colonial rule.

Quit India Movement procession in Bangalore. [22]

The British government responded quickly and harshly. Public gatherings were banned. Congress leaders, including Gandhi, were arrested almost immediately. Thousands of protesters were also imprisoned. Over the course of the movement, more than 100,000 people were arrested, and hundreds of civilians lost their lives, many during clashes with British forces.

At first, the movement appeared to fail. Its leaders spent years in prison, and the protests were eventually suppressed. However, the uprising still had a deep impact. Britain had to divert troops and resources to control the unrest in India while fighting a global war. The strain added to the growing sense that British rule in India could not last forever.

In 1944, the Quit India Movement began to fade as British authorities suppressed the remaining protests. Gandhi was released from prison that year because his health had deteriorated. Even after his release, he continued to demand the freedom of other Congress leaders. Many of those leaders were finally released in 1945 as the war drew to a close.

The Indian National Army

Not every Indian who fought during the Second World War fought on Britain's side. One of the most unusual chapters of the war was the rise of the Indian National Army, led by the nationalist leader Subhas Chandra Bose.

Bose had long believed that nonviolent resistance alone would not drive the British out of India. The war gave him a chance to try a different path. He escaped British surveillance and secretly left India. After a long and dangerous journey, he reached Germany and later traveled to Japanese-controlled territory in Asia.

There, he took command of the Indian National Army, often called the INA. The force was made up mostly of Indian soldiers who had been captured by Japan in Southeast Asia. Others were Indian civilians living abroad who volunteered to fight for independence. Under Bose's leadership, the INA joined the Japanese war effort against the British.

In 1944, Japanese forces launched a major offensive toward India's northeastern frontier. The INA fought alongside them. The campaign led to the battles of Imphal and Kohima, two of the fiercest battles fought in Asia during the war.

For a time, Japanese and INA forces pushed dangerously close to breaking through Allied defenses and moving deeper into India. However, the offensive soon stalled. Allied troops eventually forced them back, resulting in a decisive victory.

The campaign ended in defeat for the INA, but the sight of Indians fighting the British under their own flag left a deep impression. It showed that the struggle for independence had taken a new and dramatic turn. For the British, it was a troubling sign that their hold over India might not last much longer.

The All-India Muslim League

Muhammad Ali Jinnah, who led the All-India Muslim League, saw the resignation of the Congress ministries in 1939 as a turning point. When the Indian National Congress stepped away from government at the start of the Second World War, it created a political opening. Jinnah believed Muslims could now play a larger role in shaping India's future.

For some time, Jinnah had been uneasy about what would happen to Muslims in a country where Hindus formed the majority. As India pushed for greater power from the British, he became increasingly convinced that most political authority would eventually fall into Hindu hands. Jinnah believed Muslims needed stronger safeguards to protect their rights and interests.

Jinnah also offered to cooperate with the British during the war. He hoped that by supporting Britain in its time of need, the Muslim League would gain greater influence in future negotiations over India's political future.

The British government, already struggling with the pressures of war, found the Muslim League easier to work with than the Indian National Congress. Congress leaders were openly challenging British rule, while the Muslim League was willing to negotiate. This situation deepened the growing divide between the two political groups.

Muhammad Ali Jinnah.[28]

After the Quit India Movement began in 1942, many Congress leaders were arrested and imprisoned. With Congress leadership out of the political arena for several years, the Muslim League had more freedom to organize and expand its support across the country.

By the end of the war, the All-India Muslim League had grown dramatically. In the elections of 1945 and 1946, the Muslim League won the overwhelming majority of seats reserved for Muslim voters. The results showed just how much support the Muslim League had gained during the war years.

Abul Kasem Fazlul Huq

Commonly known as the Lion of Bengal, or Sher-e-Bangla, A. K. Fazlul Huq had a long and remarkable political career. Over the years, he held many important positions and played a role in several major political movements in India during the early 20th century.

Huq was born into a Muslim Bengali family in the Bengal region. He later studied law in Calcutta and entered public life as a lawyer and political activist. Early in his career, he worked with the Indian National Congress, hoping to advance the cause of Indian self-rule.

A. K. Fazlul Huq.[24]

Over time, however, he began to focus more on issues affecting Muslims in India. In 1913, he became secretary of the Bengal Provincial Muslim League. During this period, it was not unusual for politicians to work with both Congress and the Muslim League, and Huq maintained ties with leaders in both organizations.

In 1916, he became general secretary of the All-India Muslim League. That same year, the Indian National Congress and the Muslim League reached an important agreement known as the Lucknow Pact, which attempted to bring the two groups closer together in their efforts to secure political reforms from the British.

After the Government of India Act of 1919 introduced the system of diarchy, Huq entered the provincial government and served as Bengal's education minister. The experience gave him valuable political influence and strengthened his reputation among voters.

His greatest rise to power came after the provincial elections held under the Government of India Act of 1935. In 1937, Huq became the first prime minister of Bengal. He formed a coalition government led by the party he founded, the Krishak Praja Party. The name of the party meant "farmer and tenant." Its goal was to improve the lives of peasants and rural workers. Huq believed the existing system unfairly favored wealthy landowners while farmers struggled with heavy debts. During his time in office, his government passed measures that helped reduce peasant debt and limited the power of large landlords, known as zamindars.

Huq remained prime minister of Bengal from April 1937 until March 1943. These years were a turbulent time in India. Britain had entered another world war and had drawn India into the conflict. At the same time, nationalist sentiment continued to grow across the country. Tensions between Hindu and Muslim political groups also began to rise as the debate over India's future intensified.

In 1940, Huq played a key role in a historic moment in Indian politics. At a meeting of the Muslim League in Lahore, he introduced a resolution calling for independent Muslim-majority states in parts of India. The proposal later became known as the Lahore Resolution, and it laid the foundation for the future creation of Pakistan.

For a time, Huq worked closely with Muhammad Ali Jinnah and the Muslim League. His popularity among rural voters in Bengal helped expand political support for Muslim leaders and their demands. However, the relationship between Huq and Jinnah eventually deteriorated, and Huq later broke with the Muslim League.

Even so, his influence on politics in Bengal and his role in shaping the debates that led to the creation of Pakistan left a lasting mark on the region's history.

Lahore Resolution of 1940

One of Fazlul Huq's most important contributions to the Pakistan movement was the Lahore Resolution, later often called the Pakistan Resolution.

The idea behind the resolution had been growing for years. Muslim leaders had long tried to protect Muslim interests through political safeguards such as separate electorates and greater autonomy for Muslim-majority provinces. However, many in the Muslim League had come to believe that these measures were no longer enough. In a country where Hindus formed the majority, they feared Muslim political power would always remain limited.

By the late 1930s, more leaders in the All-India Muslim League began to argue that Muslims needed their own political homeland. The idea slowly gained support among Muslims across India. With this goal in mind, Muslim League leaders prepared a resolution to clarify their demands. The proposal called for independent Muslim-majority states in the northwestern and eastern regions of India.

The resolution was presented by A. K. Fazlul Huq during the Muslim League's annual session held in Lahore from March 22nd to March 24th, 1940. The meeting took place at what was then known as Minto Park, today called Iqbal Park.

The All-India Muslim League Working Committee, Lahore session, March 1940.[25]

The proposal received strong support from the Muslim League's leadership and was passed during the session. The Lahore Resolution soon became the foundation for the demand that would eventually lead to the creation of Pakistan.

After the resolution was adopted, Muhammad Ali Jinnah's leadership within the Muslim League grew even stronger. Many Muslims across India increasingly looked to him to turn the idea of a Muslim homeland into reality.

Indian National Congress leaders strongly rejected the resolution. Figures such as Gandhi and Nehru argued that dividing the country along religious lines would only create deeper divisions. They insisted that India's struggle for independence required unity between Hindus and Muslims.

It is important to remember that not all Muslims supported the idea of partition. Many Muslim leaders still believed that India should remain a single united country. One of the groups that opposed the creation of Pakistan was the All India Azad Muslim Conference, which brought together several Muslim organizations that favored a united India.

Soon after the Lahore Resolution, the Azad Muslim Conference met in Delhi and declared its support for an independent but united India without religious division.

Tensions between different political groups continued to grow in the years that followed. The war, the weakening of British authority, and the deepening divide between Congress and the Muslim League created a political climate that pushed the question of partition closer to reality.

India and World War II

After Lord Linlithgow declared India at war with Germany, the country once again found itself drawn into a global conflict. Soldiers, food, and money were redirected to support Britain's war effort.

When the war began in 1939, the British Indian Army had roughly 200,000 soldiers. By the end of the war in 1945, that number had grown to about 2.5 million. It became the largest volunteer army in history. Indians served in the army, navy, and air force, making India one of the largest contributors to the Allied war effort.

Over the six years of war, more than 2.5 million Indian soldiers fought alongside British forces against Germany and its allies. Indian troops were sent to many parts of the world, including Africa, Italy, and the Middle East. They took part in several major campaigns and battles.

Indian forces also played an important role in the war against Japan. Fighting in the jungles of Burma and along India's eastern frontier helped stop Japanese forces from advancing further into the region.

India also became a major Allied base during the war. The country played a key role in the China-Burma-India theater, supporting China's struggle against Japan. Supplies were flown over the Himalayas in dangerous missions known as the "Hump" airlift. The Allies also built the Ledo Road through Burma to move equipment and supplies into China.

Unlike during the First World War, many Indians were not eager to support Britain in another costly conflict. Leaders in the Indian National Congress strongly objected to India being dragged into the war without consultation. They tried to negotiate with Britain, offering support for the war in exchange for independence, but Britain refused to make such a promise.

Despite the Indian National Congress's opposition, the war effort continued. Britain continued to rely heavily on India for soldiers, money, and industrial production. India's location and its large army were crucial in preventing a Japanese invasion of the subcontinent.

As with most wars, the cost was high. More than eighty-seven thousand Indian soldiers lost their lives. Thousands more were wounded or never returned home.

The war also brought hardship to civilians. Britain drew heavily on India's resources, and the strain was felt across the country. Prices rose sharply, and many goods became scarce. For ordinary people, everyday life became more difficult.

The situation grew even worse in 1943 when a devastating famine struck Bengal. The Bengal Famine of 1943 killed between two and three million people. The British government's response to the crisis was widely criticized as slow and inadequate. Food and shipping were still being directed toward the war effort while millions of people struggled to survive.

Despite the suffering, the war years also brought important changes to India. The demands of wartime production forced industries to expand. Factories began producing weapons, ammunition, uniforms, and other supplies needed for the war. Steel, textiles, and other industries grew rapidly during these years.

By the end of the war, India's economy had been transformed. Industrial production had expanded, and the country had developed a much larger manufacturing base than before.

The war also changed the global balance of power. When the fighting ended, Britain was exhausted both economically and politically. Maintaining control over a vast empire became far more difficult.

At the same time, the United States emerged as the dominant power in the world. Britain, once the center of a global empire, now faced the difficult task of rebuilding its own country after years of war. In this new reality, holding on to India became increasingly unsustainable. Anti-colonial movements were growing stronger, and Britain no longer had the same power or resources to suppress them.

In the decades that followed, many other colonies around the world would also gain independence as the great age of European empires came to an end.

Chapter 9: Partition, Independence, and Legacy

The Second World War marked a decisive turning point in India's path to independence and accelerated the decline of the British Empire. Decades of protests, civil disobedience movements, and the Quit India Movement had pushed the independence struggle to a point where it could no longer be ignored.

By the time the war officially ended on September 2nd, 1945, Indian leaders and the wider public knew they could not step back from their demand for self-rule. Britain, exhausted by years of war and facing growing unrest in India, also understood that maintaining control was becoming increasingly difficult. The question was no longer whether India would become independent but how Britain would manage its withdrawal.

The independence movement, led by figures from both the Indian National Congress and the All-India Muslim League, including Jawaharlal Nehru, Mahatma Gandhi, and Muhammad Ali Jinnah, continued to push harder for freedom.

Indian Navy Mutiny

The period between the end of the war and India gaining independence was marked by several dramatic events that unfolded in quick succession. One of the most significant was a naval uprising that began in Bombay.

Many Indian servicemen were deeply frustrated by their treatment under British command. During the war, Indian troops had fought around the world alongside British forces. Yet they were often treated as second-class soldiers and faced racism, poor living conditions, and unequal pay. Many also believed that Britain was deliberately delaying real political reforms and independence.

Before the war, the Royal Indian Navy was a small force of only a few thousand men. When the conflict began, the British rapidly expanded it to meet wartime demands. By 1945, the navy had grown to around twenty thousand sailors. Many of these recruits came from rural areas and joined for steady pay during a time of rising prices and economic hardship. During the war, the navy helped escort convoys, patrol the seas, and protect shipping across the Indian Ocean.

When the war ended, many sailors expected conditions to improve. Instead, they found themselves living in cramped quarters, dealing with poor food and harsh treatment from British officers while waiting to be demobilized. Frustration and resentment continued to grow.

Tensions were further inflamed by the trials of soldiers from the Indian National Army. These men, who had fought alongside Japan against the British under the leadership of Subhas Chandra Bose, were captured and put on trial for treason at the Red Fort in Delhi between 1945 and 1946. The trials drew enormous public attention. Many Indians viewed the defendants not as traitors but as patriots who had fought for the country's freedom. Demonstrations and protests spread across the country.

British officials became increasingly worried about what this meant for the loyalty of the Indian armed forces. Sympathy for the INA soldiers spread even among men who had served on Britain's side during the war. Memories of the great uprising of 1857, when Indian soldiers had turned against British rule, still lingered in the minds of colonial authorities.

The naval mutiny began against this tense background on February 18th, 1946. It started at HMIS Talwar, a naval signal training establishment in Bombay. Sailors there refused to report for duty, protesting poor food and discriminatory treatment by British officers.

The strike spread quickly. Within days, thousands of naval ratings (the enlisted sailors of the Royal Indian Navy) joined the protest. The unrest spread to dozens of ships and shore establishments across several cities, including Karachi and Calcutta. In Bombay, around ten thousand sailors took part in demonstrations. British flags were torn down and replaced with nationalist flags representing different political groups in India.

Violence soon broke out in the city. Shops were attacked, transport was disrupted, and clashes erupted between protesters and British forces. Troops were deployed, and gunfire was used to restore order. By the time the unrest subsided, more than two hundred people had been killed in Bombay. Many more were injured.

Despite the scale of the uprising, the mutiny did not receive support from India's major political leaders. Gandhi strongly condemned the violence, and both the Indian National Congress and Muslim League leaders urged the sailors to surrender.

By February 23rd, 1946, the mutiny had come to an end. Although it was brief and ultimately unsuccessful, it sent a powerful message. The uprising showed British authorities that even the armed forces could no longer be fully relied upon to uphold colonial rule.

In a symbolic sense, the event also echoed the beginning of the independence struggle. Nearly ninety years earlier, the revolt of Indian soldiers in 1857 had shaken British rule in India. Now, in the final phase of the freedom movement, another military uprising had once again challenged British authority.

1946 Elections

Another important event took place shortly before independence: the provincial elections held between 1945 and 1946. The results mattered enormously, as they would decide who controlled the provincial governments and which parties would help shape India's future constitution.

During the campaign, the growing divide between Hindus and Muslims became impossible to ignore. The Indian National Congress continued to present itself as a party for all Indians, but most of its support came from Hindu voters. The All-India Muslim League, led by Muhammad Ali Jinnah, focused on representing Muslim political interests. The idea of Pakistan, a separate Muslim homeland, became one of the main issues of the election.

In total, 1,585 seats were contested across the provincial legislatures. Congress won 923 seats, giving it a strong overall majority. However, the most important result came from the seats reserved for Muslim voters.

Of the 482 Muslim seats, the Muslim League won 425. The outcome strengthened Jinnah's claim that the Muslim League was the only party that truly represented India's Muslim population.

A few months after the elections, the British government sent a group of officials to India known as the Cabinet Mission. Their task was to find a way to transfer power while keeping the country united. The plan they proposed called for a single Indian union with a limited central government responsible mainly for defense, foreign affairs, and communications. Most other powers would remain with the provinces.

The provinces would also be grouped into larger regional blocs. Muslim-majority provinces in the northwest and northeast would be placed together, giving them greater influence over their own affairs. Under this plan, the creation of a separate and fully independent Pakistan would be rejected.

At first, both the Indian National Congress and the Muslim League were willing to consider the proposal. Jinnah was not completely opposed to a united India if Muslim-majority regions were given enough political protection and authority. However, distrust between the two parties ran deep, and the negotiations quickly became tense.

The situation worsened in July 1946. Jawaharlal Nehru announced that although Congress would take part in the new constitutional process, it did not consider itself bound by every detail of the Cabinet Mission Plan and could make changes later if necessary. Jinnah saw this as confirmation of his fears. If Congress eventually controlled the government, he believed it would reshape the system in its favor and leave Muslims politically vulnerable.

Viewing Nehru's statement as a betrayal, Jinnah withdrew the Muslim League's support for the plan and warned that the Muslim League would begin a struggle to force Britain to accept its demands.

Direct Action Day

On August 16ᵗʰ, 1946, the Muslim League launched what it called Direct Action Day. The announcement came only weeks after Muhammad Ali Jinnah withdrew the Muslim League's support for the Cabinet Mission Plan. Frustrated with the political deadlock, the Muslim League called on Muslims across India to take direct action to press Britain to accept the demand for a separate Muslim state.

The call was meant to include strikes, protests, and mass demonstrations. But in the city of Calcutta, where tensions between

Hindus and Muslims had already been rising, events quickly spiraled out of control. Large crowds gathered for rallies and demonstrations throughout the city. Calcutta had declared a public holiday, which brought even more people into the streets. Before long, clashes broke out between Hindu and Muslim groups. What began as political demonstrations soon turned into widespread communal violence.

For several days, the city descended into chaos. Armed mobs attacked neighborhoods, shops were looted, and homes were set on fire. The fighting spread through the city's streets and crowded districts. Police and authorities struggled to restore order.

The victims of the 1946 riots in Calcutta.[26]

By the time the violence ended a few days later, the scale of the destruction was staggering. More than four thousand people had been killed, and thousands more were injured. An estimated 100,000 residents fled their homes to escape the violence. Entire neighborhoods were left damaged or destroyed.

The events became known as the Great Calcutta Killings. News of the bloodshed shocked the country and deepened the growing mistrust between Hindu and Muslim communities. In the months that followed, violence continued to spread in other parts of the country. Each new outbreak made the prospect of partition seem more likely.

Partition and Independence

Less than a year after Direct Action Day, a new viceroy arrived in India. In March 1947, Louis Mountbatten was sent to oversee Britain's final withdrawal from the country. He would be the last man to hold the position.

The situation he inherited was already spiraling out of control. Violence was spreading, and relations between the Indian National Congress and the All-India Muslim League had completely broken down. Britain, exhausted after the Second World War, was eager to leave.

The British government had originally planned to transfer power by June 1948. Mountbatten quickly decided that waiting that long was dangerous. He pushed the timetable forward dramatically. Instead of June 1948, Britain would leave in August 1947. The decision left very little time to prepare for the enormous task of dividing the country.

Within a few months of arriving, Mountbatten reached a difficult conclusion. Keeping India united no longer seemed possible. On June 3rd, 1947, he announced a plan to divide British India into two separate states, India and Pakistan. The proposal later became law when the British Parliament passed the Indian Independence Act 1947 in July 1947. The act created two new dominions within the British Commonwealth.

Pakistan was formed from Muslim-majority regions. In the west, it included West Punjab, Sindh, the North-West Frontier Province, and Balochistan. In the east, it included East Bengal. This arrangement created two separate wings of Pakistan (West Pakistan and East Pakistan), which were divided by more than a thousand miles of Indian territory.

The act also affected the many princely states scattered across the subcontinent. These 565 states had previously been tied to Britain through treaties. With the end of British rule, those agreements were dissolved. Each ruler was now free to decide whether to join India or Pakistan.

Most princely states eventually joined India. A few cases proved far more complicated. The state of Jammu and Kashmir delayed its decision. Its ruler, Hari Singh, hoped the state could remain independent. That plan collapsed in October 1947 when armed fighters from Pakistan entered the region, and fighting broke out. Facing invasion, the ruler asked India for military help and agreed to join the country. The crisis sparked the first war between India and Pakistan.

Two other states also created disputes. In Junagadh, a Muslim ruler governed a mostly Hindu population. The ruler chose to join Pakistan, which angered many residents and leaders in India. The issue was later settled through a plebiscite in February 1948. Most voters chose to join India.

Hyderabad State tried to remain independent under its ruler, Osman Ali Khan, Asaf Jah VII. Negotiations dragged on for months while unrest grew inside the state. In September 1948, India sent in troops and quickly took control. Hyderabad was then incorporated into India.

Once the plan for independence was finalized, the British Parliament approved it, and King George VI granted it royal assent. August 15th, 1947, was chosen as the official date when British rule in India would end.

Nehru, India's first prime minister, addresses a newly independent nation on August 15th, 1947.[37]

After nearly two centuries under British control, India had finally reached the end of its long struggle for independence. On August 15th, 1947, the country became a sovereign nation. The leader of the Indian National Congress, Jawaharlal Nehru, became India's first prime minister. He had worked closely with Mahatma Gandhi for many years and was widely seen as one of the most important leaders of the independence movement.

Although British rule had ended, the transition did not happen overnight. The last British viceroy, Mountbatten, remained in India for some time as the country's first governor-general to help oversee the transfer of power.

Today, August 15th is celebrated each year as India's Independence Day.

Consequences of Partition

By the time partition was finally agreed upon, many leaders had come to believe that keeping India united was no longer possible. Years of political conflict, rising distrust between communities, and growing violence had pushed the country to the brink. Had Britain refused to divide the country, a full civil war very well might have broken out.

Even so, the decision to divide India came at an enormous cost.

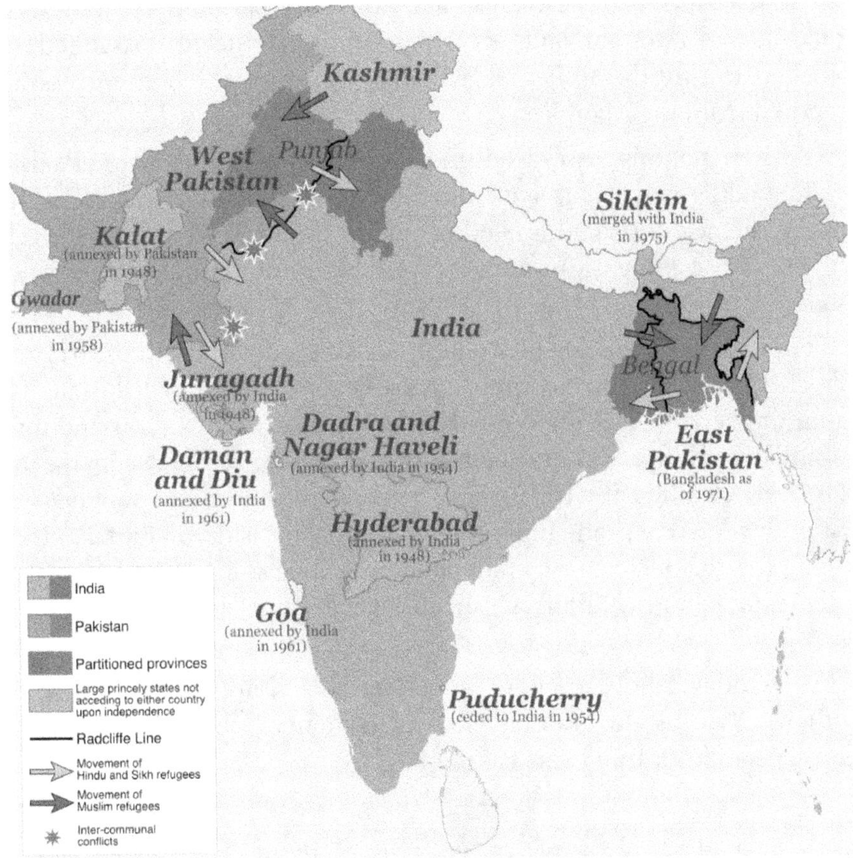

Map of the Partition of India in 1947.

Partition was carried out with remarkable speed. The timetable for British withdrawal had been moved forward, leaving very little time to prepare for the complicated task of dividing a country of hundreds of millions of people. New borders were drawn in a matter of weeks.

Once those borders were announced, one of the largest migrations in human history began. Between twelve and fifteen million people were forced to leave their homes. Hindus and Sikhs fled areas that became part of Pakistan, while Muslims moved toward the new Muslim state.

The journey was often chaotic and dangerous. Entire communities packed their belongings and set out on foot, by train, or by cart in search of safety. Armed groups attacked villages and refugee columns. Trains carrying refugees sometimes arrived at their destinations filled with the dead.

Historians estimate that between 200,000 and one million people were killed during the violence that followed partition. Hundreds of thousands of women and children were abducted, assaulted, or trafficked during the upheaval. Millions more were left homeless and separated from their families.

The new nations also faced enormous political challenges. Pakistan had to build many of its government institutions while dealing with a massive refugee crisis and limited resources. India faced its own struggles as it worked to unite a vast and diverse country under a new democratic system.

Tensions between the two nations continued to shape the region's politics. One of the most complicated issues involved East Pakistan. The region was separated from West Pakistan by more than a thousand miles of Indian territory. Cultural and political differences between the two sides grew steadily. By 1971, those tensions erupted into war between East and West Pakistan. India intervened on the side of East Pakistan, helping the region secure its independence. The war led to the creation of the new nation of Bangladesh, though it came at a terrible human cost.

Even today, the legacy of partition still shapes relations across southern Asia, as the trauma of displacement, violence, and loss left deep scars in both India and Pakistan.

Legacy of the British Raj

What is the legacy of the British Raj? It is a question historians and scholars still debate today. Based on the events described in the previous chapters, it would be easy to say that its legacy is one of violence, discrimination, and bloodshed. The end of British rule also led to the division of the subcontinent into separate nations that still struggle with the consequences of partition. However, the story is not quite that simple.

Many historians describe the legacy of British rule as complicated. On the one hand, the British Empire extracted enormous wealth and resources from India. Taxes, trade policies, and colonial administration helped transfer wealth to Britain for generations. Some economists have tried to estimate the scale of that loss. One estimate by Utsa Patnaik suggests that Britain extracted wealth worth as much as forty-five trillion dollars between 1765 and 1938, though many historians debate the methods used to reach that number.

Symbols of the empire still spark debate today. One example is the Koh-i-Noor, one of the largest cut diamonds in the world, which remains part of the British Crown Jewels. Some view it as a symbol of colonial plunder, while others point out that it was transferred to Britain under the treaties that followed the conquest of Punjab. The debate over who truly owns such artifacts continues today.

British rule also had major economic consequences in India. The rise of British industry and global trade damaged many traditional Indian industries, especially textiles. Many artisans and skilled workers lost their livelihoods as cheaper machine-made goods flooded the market. At the same time, colonial rule helped build new cities and administrative centers. Railways, ports, and expanding trade created new opportunities for merchants, clerks, and professionals. Over time, this helped give rise to a growing educated middle class.

Social reforms also took place during the colonial period. The British government banned practices such as sati and supported efforts to expand education for women. However, many of these reforms were also strongly promoted by Indian social reformers who pushed for change within their own society.

British rule introduced institutions that continue to shape India today. The legal system, civil service, parliamentary government, and widespread use of the English language all developed during this period and remain part of India's public life.

At the same time, colonial policies often deepened political and religious divisions. British officials sometimes encouraged separate political representation for different communities. Over time, tensions between Hindus and Muslims grew more intense. These divisions played an important role in the events that eventually led to partition. Relations between India and Pakistan have remained tense ever since, shaped by the memories of partition and ongoing disputes such as the conflict over Kashmir.

Because of all these factors, it is difficult to say with certainty whether India today is better or worse off because of its colonial past. Some of the institutions and infrastructure introduced during British rule became part of modern India's development. At the same time, the economic disruption, political divisions, and violence of the colonial era left deep scars that are still felt today.

The legacy of the British Raj, like the empire itself, remains complex. It is a history shaped by exploitation and reform, conflict and change, and loss and transformation. Understanding that legacy remains an important part of modern South Asia.

Chapter 10: Agents of Change

India would not be the country it is today without the dedication and support of millions of people who fought hard to gain freedom for the country, often at great cost to themselves. It took two centuries, but they continued to fight for what they wanted, and through the sacrifice and dedication of millions of people, they got there.

While we discussed some key figures in detail already, such as Gandhi and Lord Ripon, a history of the British Raj would not be complete without mentioning a few other influential figures, both British and Indian, who contributed greatly to the cause of independence.

Subhas Chandra Bose

Subhas Chandra Bose was born on January 23rd, 1897, in Cuttack in what is now the Indian state of Odisha. He came from a prominent and well-educated Bengali family. Bose later became one of the most famous and controversial figures of India's independence movement. Many supporters affectionately called him Netaji, meaning "Respected Leader."

He was educated in India before traveling to England to continue his studies at the University of Cambridge. His family hoped he would join the prestigious Indian

Subhas Chandra Bose.[29]

Civil Service. Bose passed the difficult exam in 1920, but instead of accepting the position, he resigned before taking the job and returned to India. He believed his duty was to help fight for the country's independence.

Back in India, Bose joined the nationalist movement and became involved in the Non-Cooperation Movement led by Mahatma Gandhi. His activism quickly brought him into conflict with the colonial authorities, and he spent several years in prison.

Bose rose rapidly within the Indian National Congress. In 1927, he and Jawaharlal Nehru were both appointed general secretaries of the party.

By the 1930s, however, Bose and Gandhi began to disagree strongly about how independence should be achieved. Gandhi believed in nonviolent resistance and civil disobedience. Bose believed the struggle should be more forceful and that Britain might only leave if it was pushed out by stronger action.

During this time, Bose traveled to Europe several times, partly for health reasons. While there, he tried to draw international attention to India's struggle for independence. In 1937, he married Emilie Schenkl. The marriage was kept largely private because Bose believed it might harm his political career.

Tensions within the Indian National Congress eventually reached a breaking point. After disagreements with other leaders, Bose resigned from the party's leadership and formed the All India Forward Bloc, which pushed for more radical action against British rule.

The British government soon placed Bose under house arrest. In January 1941, he escaped and secretly left India. After a long journey through Afghanistan and the Soviet Union, he arrived in Germany, where he sought support from Britain's enemies during the Second World War.

Later in the war, Bose traveled to Southeast Asia, where Japan had captured thousands of Indian soldiers fighting for the British. Some of these prisoners agreed to join a force that would fight for India's independence. This force became known as the Indian National Army, or INA. The army had originally been formed earlier in the war, but Bose reorganized and expanded it into a much larger fighting force.

In 1943, Bose announced the creation of the Provisional Government of Free India, also known as Azad Hind. Several Axis countries recognized the government, and Japan handed over control of the Andaman and Nicobar Islands to it. Bose hoped this would serve as the foundation for an independent Indian state.

With Japanese support, the INA advanced toward India through Burma in 1944. For a moment, it seemed possible that Bose's forces might reach Indian territory. However, the campaign collapsed. Japanese supply lines were weak, and Allied forces pushed the attackers back during the battles of Imphal and Kohima. The INA was forced to retreat.

The situation changed completely in August 1945 after the atomic bombings of Hiroshima and Nagasaki. With Japan defeated, the INA collapsed as well.

Bose attempted to escape the advancing Allied forces. According to the most widely accepted account, he died in a plane crash in Taiwan on August 18th, 1945. However, rumors and conspiracy theories about his fate have continued for decades.

After the war, several officers of the INA were put on trial for treason at the Red Fort in Delhi. The trials produced the opposite effect that the British had hoped for. Instead of weakening the independence movement, they stirred up enormous public sympathy for the accused soldiers. Protests spread across India, and many people began to see the INA soldiers as patriots who had fought for freedom.

Bose remains one of the most debated figures in India's struggle for independence. His determination and leadership inspired many Indians, but his decision to seek help from Nazi Germany and Imperial Japan continues to generate controversy. What cannot be denied is that he devoted his life to one goal: the independence of India. Unfortunately for him, he did not live to see it achieved.

Annie Besant

Annie Besant is best known for her role in the Indian Home Rule movement. She is also a powerful example of how people from very different backgrounds became involved in India's struggle for independence.

Besant was born Annie Wood in London on October 1st, 1847. Over the course of her life, she became many things, including a social reformer, a writer, a lecturer, and eventually a political activist. What made her especially unusual was that she was a white British woman who became deeply involved in the movement for Indian self-rule.

In 1867, she married Frank Besant. The marriage did not last. The two separated in 1873, which was highly unusual at the time. After the separation, Besant moved away from the religious beliefs she had grown up with and became involved in secular and radical political circles.

Annie Besant.[80]

During these years, she became known as a passionate campaigner for social reform. She spoke openly about women's rights, supported birth control, and argued that women should have access to education and the right to vote. Her outspoken views made her both famous and controversial in Britain.

Besant's life changed again when she joined the Theosophical Society, a movement that promoted spiritual ideas drawn from both Eastern and Western traditions. Her work with the society eventually brought her to India in 1893.

India quickly became the center of her life. She settled there and became deeply involved in the country's political and social issues. In 1907, she was elected president of the Theosophical Society, whose international headquarters was in India.

As her interest in Indian affairs grew, so did her support for self-government. In 1916, Besant joined forces with Bal Gangadhar Tilak to promote the Home Rule movement, which called for India to govern itself while remaining part of the British Empire. Through speeches, newspapers, and political organizing, Besant helped spread nationalist ideas across the country.

Her influence reached its peak in 1917 when she became president of the Indian National Congress. She was the first woman ever to hold that position.

Annie Besant and Gandhi in Madras.[81]

As new leaders such as Gandhi began to take a larger role in the independence struggle, Besant gradually stepped back from the center of politics. She still continued to write, lecture, and advocate for Indian self-rule, both in India and during speaking tours in Britain.

Besant remained active in public life for many years. She died on September 20th, 1933, at the age of eighty-five in Madras (now Chennai). Following Hindu custom, her body was cremated.

Today, Annie Besant is remembered for many things—her advocacy for women's rights, her work with the Theosophical Society, and her support for India's struggle for self-government. Though she was born in Britain, she devoted much of her life to India and its people.

Thomas Baring, 1st Earl of Northbrook

Thomas George Baring was born on January 22nd, 1826, in England. He came from the wealthy and influential Baring family, which had made its fortune in banking. Although his family was powerful, he was not born into the aristocracy. Later in life, he was given the title Earl of Northbrook.

As a young man, Baring entered public service. He worked as a private secretary to several British officials before moving into government positions of his own. Over time, he served in roles such as civil lord of the admiralty and under-secretary of state for India.

In 1848, he married Elizabeth Sturt. The couple had three children together. Elizabeth died in 1867, and Baring never remarried.

Baring's career took a dramatic turn in 1872. That year, the sitting viceroy of India, Richard Bourke, was assassinated in the Andaman Islands. Soon afterward, British Prime Minister William Ewart Gladstone chose Baring to replace him.

Baring arrived in India at a difficult time. Poverty was widespread, and many people were struggling under taxes and economic pressure. Compared with many other colonial officials, Baring preferred a more moderate style of rule. He believed stability and careful administration were the best way to govern. During his time in office, he supported free trade and worked to reduce some import duties that he believed were hurting commerce.

Painting of Thomas George Baring, 1st Earl of Northbrook.[89]

One of the biggest tests of his leadership came in 1873 when famine threatened eastern India. Food shortages began to spread across Bihar. Baring responded quickly. He ordered large shipments of rice to be brought in from Burma and organized relief efforts to distribute food. The relief effort cost the government a great deal of money, but it helped prevent a much larger disaster. Some officials in Britain later criticized him for spending too much on famine relief.

Baring's moderate policies often brought him into conflict with officials in London. By 1876, he was arguing frequently with Foreign Secretary Robert Gascoyne-Cecil over foreign policy and the direction of British rule in India. The disagreements eventually led Baring to resign as viceroy. He was replaced by Edward Robert Lytton, whose rule took a far harsher approach.

Although Baring did not change the structure of British rule, his time in office is often remembered for its more cautious policies and his willingness to spend money to prevent famine. Today, his name still appears on several colonial-era buildings, including the Northbrook Clock Tower in Lahore and Northbrook Hall in Dhaka.

Khudadad Khan

Khudadad Khan was born in 1888 in Punjab, in what is now Pakistan. He holds the distinction of being the first Indian and the first Muslim to receive the Victoria Cross, the British Empire's highest award for valor.

Khan served as a sepoy in the British Indian Army with the 129th Duke of Connaught's Own Baluchis. When the First World War began in 1914, his battalion was sent to Europe to fight alongside British troops on the Western Front.

That same year, his unit took part in the First Battle of Ypres. The fighting was fierce and chaotic. German forces were pressing hard against the Allied lines. Khan was part of a machine-gun team defending a critical position. As the battle intensified, members of the gun crew were killed or wounded one by one.

Despite being badly injured himself, Khan continued to operate the machine gun and fire at the advancing enemy. Eventually, the position was overrun. Khan was left for dead on the battlefield. However, he survived the night and later managed to make his way back to his regiment.

Khudadad Khan.[88]

His actions helped slow the German advance and bought valuable time for reinforcements to arrive and strengthen the line. For his extraordinary bravery, Khan was awarded the Victoria Cross. He later traveled to London, where he received the medal from King George V.

After the war, Khan remained in the army and continued his military career. He eventually retired with the rank of subedar (the second-highest rank an Indian could achieve during the British Raj).

Khan lived through many of the major events that reshaped South Asia in the 20th century. He witnessed the Second World War, the final years of the independence movement, and the partition of India in 1947. After retirement, he settled in Pakistan, where he lived quietly until his death in 1971.

Today, Khudadad Khan is remembered as one of the bravest soldiers to have served in the British Indian Army. His story is also a reminder of the thousands of Indian soldiers who fought in distant wars during the era of the British Empire, often with little recognition for their sacrifices.

Gopal Krishna Gokhale

Gopal Krishna Gokhale was one of the most important Moderate leaders in the Indian National Congress. He believed India's path to self-rule should come through patience, negotiation, and constitutional reform rather than confrontation.

Gokhale was born on May 9th, 1866, in what is now the state of Maharashtra. His family was not wealthy, but they valued education and worked hard to give him opportunities they themselves had never had.

He was fortunate to receive an English education at a time when very few Indians could. Through his studies, he was introduced to Western political ideas about democracy, liberty, and reform. These ideas would shape the way he later approached India's struggle for greater political rights.

During his early career, Gokhale came under the influence of

Gopal Krishna Gokhale.[a]

Mahadev Govind Ranade, a respected judge and social reformer. Ranade encouraged him to enter public life and helped shape his belief that gradual reform and cooperation could bring lasting change.

Through Ranade, Gokhale became involved with the Indian National Congress in 1889. Over the following years, he rose through the ranks and became one of the leading voices of the party's Moderate wing.

Not everyone agreed with his approach. Gokhale often clashed with Bal Gangadhar Tilak, who believed more confrontational methods were needed to push the British out of India. These disagreements between Moderates and more radical leaders eventually led to a split within Congress in the early 20th century.

Gokhale also played an important role in the early political life of Mahatma Gandhi. The two men met while Gandhi was still working in South Africa. When Gandhi returned to India in 1915, he looked to

Gokhale as a mentor and guide for understanding the country's political situation. Gandhi would later refer to him as his political teacher.

Gokhale did not live long enough to see India gain independence. He died in 1915 while the country was still under British rule. However, his ideas about moderation, reform, and political responsibility continued to influence the independence movement in the years that followed.

Conclusion

Whether we agree with Britain's imperial ambitions or not, it cannot be denied that the British Raj had a profound impact on India and the world at large. When the British government took over from the East India Company, there was hope in India that things would be different. In some ways, Britain's direct rule was an improvement, but in many important ways, the system remained much the same. Resources continued to flow out of India, wealth was transferred to Britain, and colonial policies often placed the needs of the empire above those of the people living in India.

British rule reshaped the country in many ways. Borders were reorganized, administrative systems changed, and economic policies altered long-standing patterns of trade and industry. Traditional ways of life were affected as new Western institutions and ideas were introduced. Many Indians faced hardship under colonial rule, including poverty, famine, and limited political power. While British officials often spoke about ideals such as civilization, democracy, and equality, these principles were applied only gradually and in very limited ways within India.

However, historians often note that the legacy of the British Raj is not entirely negative. British rule introduced railways, modern universities, new legal institutions, and a Western-style education system. These developments helped create a new educated class of Indians who began to demand greater political rights and eventually independence. In an unexpected way, British education and India's involvement in global wars helped strengthen the independence movement that ultimately brought an end to colonial rule.

Today, India is the world's largest democracy by population and a rising global power. At the same time, it continues to face serious challenges such as inequality and religious and communal tensions, some of which historians trace in part to the colonial era.

What we will never know is what India might have become without the influence of British rule. Today, parts of India, especially its major cities, still show traces of Western institutions and traditions introduced during the colonial period. The legacy of that era can be seen in the country's legal system, political institutions, and infrastructure.

When we consider India's history, it raises difficult questions. Without colonial policies that sometimes deepened divisions between communities, would the subcontinent have remained united? Would Hindus and Muslims still be living together within a single country today? Some modern economic historians estimate that Britain extracted enormous wealth from India during colonial rule, with figures reaching into the trillions in today's value. Without that loss, how different might the economies of India, Pakistan, and Bangladesh look today?

More broadly, it invites an even larger question: how might the world look today if Britain had never become a global empire?

Here's another book by Enthralling History that you might like

Free limited time bonus

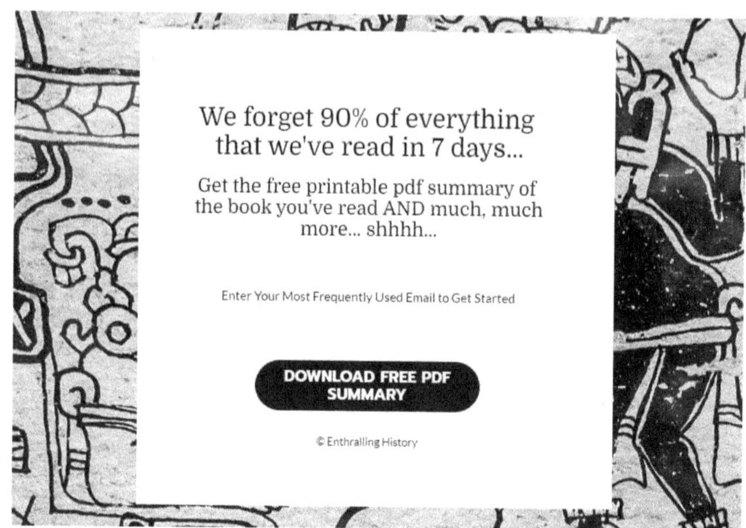

Stop for a moment. We have a free bonus set up for you. The problem is this: we forget 90% of everything that we read after 7 days. Crazy fact, right? Here's the solution: we've created a printable, 1-page pdf summary for this book that you're reading now. All you have to do to get your free pdf summary is to go to the following website:

https://livetolearn.lpages.co/enthrallinghistory/

Or, Scan the QR code!

Once you do, it will be intuitive. Enjoy, and thank you!

Sources

Ambedkar, B. R. *Annihilation of Caste*. Reprint, London: Verso, 2014.

Brown, Judith M. *Gandhi: Prisoner of Hope*. New Haven: Yale University Press, 1989.

Dalrymple, William. *The Anarchy: The East India Company, Corporate Violence, and the Pillage of an Empire*. New York: Bloomsbury Publishing, 2019.

Dalrymple, William. *The Last Mughal: The Fall of a Dynasty, Delhi, 1857*. New York: Knopf, 2007.

Davis, Mike. *Late Victorian Holocausts: El Niño Famines and the Making of the Third World*. London: Verso, 2001.

Dirks, Nicholas B. *Castes of Mind: Colonialism and the Making of Modern India*. Princeton: Princeton University Press, 2001.

Gordon, Leonard A. *Brothers Against the Raj: A Biography of Indian Nationalists Sarat and Subhas Chandra Bose*. New York: Columbia University Press, 1990.

Guha, Ramachandra. *Gandhi Before India*. New York: Knopf, 2014.

Guha, Ramachandra. *Gandhi: The Years That Changed the World, 1914–1948*. New York: Knopf, 2018.

James, Lawrence. *Raj: The Making and Unmaking of British India*. New York: St. Martin's Press, 1997.

Khan, Yasmin. *The Great Partition: The Making of India and Pakistan*. New Haven: Yale University Press, 2007.

Metcalf, Barbara D., and Thomas R. Metcalf. *A Concise History of Modern India*. 3rd ed. Cambridge: Cambridge University Press, 2012.

Raghavan, Srinath. *India's War: The Making of Modern South Asia, 1939–1945.* New York: Basic Books, 2016.

Roy, Tirthankar. *The Economic History of India, 1857–1947.* 3rd ed. Oxford: Oxford University Press, 2011.

Tharoor, Shashi. *Inglorious Empire: What the British Did to India.* London: Hurst & Company, 2017.

Tunzelmann, Alex von. *Indian Summer: The Secret History of the End of an Empire.* New York: Henry Holt, 2007.

Wolpert, Stanley. *Tilak and Gokhale: Revolution and Reform in the Making of Modern India.* Berkeley: University of California Press, 1962.

Image Sources

1 Vadac, CC BY-SA 2.5 <https://creativecommons.org/licenses/by-sa/2.5>, via Wikimedia Commons, https://commons.wikimedia.org/wiki/File:Anachronous_map_of_the_British_Empire.png

2 See page for author, CC BY-SA 4.0 <https://creativecommons.org/licenses/by-sa/4.0>, via Wikimedia Commons, https://commons.wikimedia.org/wiki/File:Coat_of_Arms_of_East_India_Company_%281600-1709%29.svg

3 https://commons.wikimedia.org/wiki/File:Fort_St._George,_Chennai.jpg

4 https://commons.wikimedia.org/wiki/File:Two_Seapoy_Officers;_A_Private_Seapoy.jpg

5 https://commons.wikimedia.org/wiki/File:Capture_of_Delhi,_1857..jpg

6 https://commons.wikimedia.org/wiki/File:Dalhousie.jpg

7 https://commons.wikimedia.org/wiki/File:First_Train_of_East_Indian_Railway-1854.jpg

8 https://commons.wikimedia.org/wiki/File:India-famine-family-crop-420.jpg

9 https://commons.wikimedia.org/wiki/File:Robert_Bulwer-Lytton_by_Nadar.jpg

10 https://commons.wikimedia.org/wiki/File:Marquess_of_Ripon.jpg

11 Giveaway285, CC BY-SA 4.0 <https://creativecommons.org/licenses/by-sa/4.0>, via Wikimedia Commons; https://commons.wikimedia.org/wiki/File:Indian_Caste_System.jpg

12 https://commons.wikimedia.org/wiki/File:Dr._Bhimrao_Ambedkar.jpg

13 https://commons.wikimedia.org/wiki/File:A_O_Hume.jpg

14 https://commons.wikimedia.org/wiki/File:1st_INC1885.jpg

15 https://commons.wikimedia.org/wiki/File:Natal_Indian_Congress.jpg

16 https://commons.wikimedia.org/wiki/File:NehruAddressingCrowds_
FatehMaidan.jpg

17 https://commons.wikimedia.org/wiki/File:Marche_sel.jpg

18 https://commons.wikimedia.org/wiki/File:Mahatma-Gandhi,_studio,_1931.jpg

19 https://commons.wikimedia.org/wiki/File:Indian_bicycle_troops_Somme_
1916_IWM_Q_3983.jpg

20 https://commons.wikimedia.org/wiki/File:Bal_Gangadhar_Tilak_in_
Madras_1917.jpg

21 https://commons.wikimedia.org/wiki/File:Victor_Hope,_2nd_Marquess_
of_Linlithgow.jpg

22 No machine-readable author provided. Dore chakravarty~commonswiki assumed
(based on copyright claims)., CC BY-SA 2.5
<https://creativecommons.org/licenses/by-sa/2.5>, via Wikimedia Commons;
https://commons.wikimedia.org/wiki/File:Procession_at_Bangalore_during_Quit_I
ndia_movement,_by_Indian_National_Congress_(1).jpg

23 https://commons.wikimedia.org/wiki/File:Jinnah1945c.jpg

24 https://commons.wikimedia.org/wiki/File:A_k_fazlul_hoque.jpg

25 https://commons.wikimedia.org/wiki/File:All_India_Muslim_League_
Working_Committee_Lahore_1940.jpg

26 https://commons.wikimedia.org/wiki/File:Calcutta_1946_riot.jpg

27 https://commons.wikimedia.org/wiki/File:PM_Nehru_addresses_the_
nation_from_the_Red_Fort_on_15_August_1947.jpg

28 Own work, CC BY-SA 4.0 <https://creativecommons.org/licenses/by-sa/4.0>, via
Wikimedia Commons; https://commons.wikimedia.org/wiki/File:Partition_
of_India_1947_en.svg

29 https://commons.wikimedia.org/wiki/File:Subhas_Chandra_Bose_NRB.jpg

30 https://commons.wikimedia.org/wiki/File:Annie_Besant_-_portrait.jpg

31 https://commons.wikimedia.org/wiki/File:Gandhi_besant_madras1921.jpg

32 https://commons.wikimedia.org/wiki/File:Arthur_Stockdale_Cope_-
_Thomas_George_Baring,_Earl_of_Northbrook.jpg

33 Unknown author, CC BY-SA 4.0 <https://creativecommons.org/licenses/by-sa/4.0>,
via Wikimedia Commons; https://commons.wikimedia.org/wiki/File:
Khudadad_Khan_VC.jpg

34 https://commons.wikimedia.org/wiki/File:GKGokhale.jpg